104

Bible Puzzles for Tweens

104 Bible Puzzles for Tweens

No further reproduction or distribution of this material is allowed without the written consent of Abingdon Press, 201 Eighth Avenue South, P.O. Box 801, Nashville, TN 37202; fax 615-749-6128; e-mail *permissions@abingdonpress.com*.

Writer/Compiler: Marcia Stoner
Cover: Keitha Vincent
Additional Credits: p. 144

ISBN 978-0-687-65056-9

08 09 10 11 12 13 14 15 16 17 — 10 9 8 7 6 5 4 3 2 1

Manufactured in the United States of America

Contents

How to Use This Book

For arrival or additional activities for any curriculum
• These puzzles can be used for arrival activities to supplement any Bible curriculum. Use the Topical and Scriptural indexes to find the puzzle that applies to what your tweens are doing.

For a nine-month Bible survey
• If you are doing a school-year overview of the Bible with your tweens, you will find puzzles for most of the topics you will cover. You would mainly use the puzzles labeled 1-78 for the first thirty-nine weeks (two puzzles per week).

For a twelve-month Bible survey
• If you are doing a twelve-month overview of the Bible with your tweens, you will find puzzles for most of the topics you will cover. The additional summer puzzles beginning on page 89 may be used in two ways:

1. Strictly for additional topics for summer. (Because so many tweens are in and out of class in the summer months, you probably will not want to leave most of the New Testament work to summer.)

2. At the appropriate place where they fall within the Bible. If you are unsure where that would be, see the Scripture Index on page 142. Those Scriptures with ** preceding them in the index are the additional summer puzzles. They are listed in the index in the order that their Scripture references appear in the Bible.

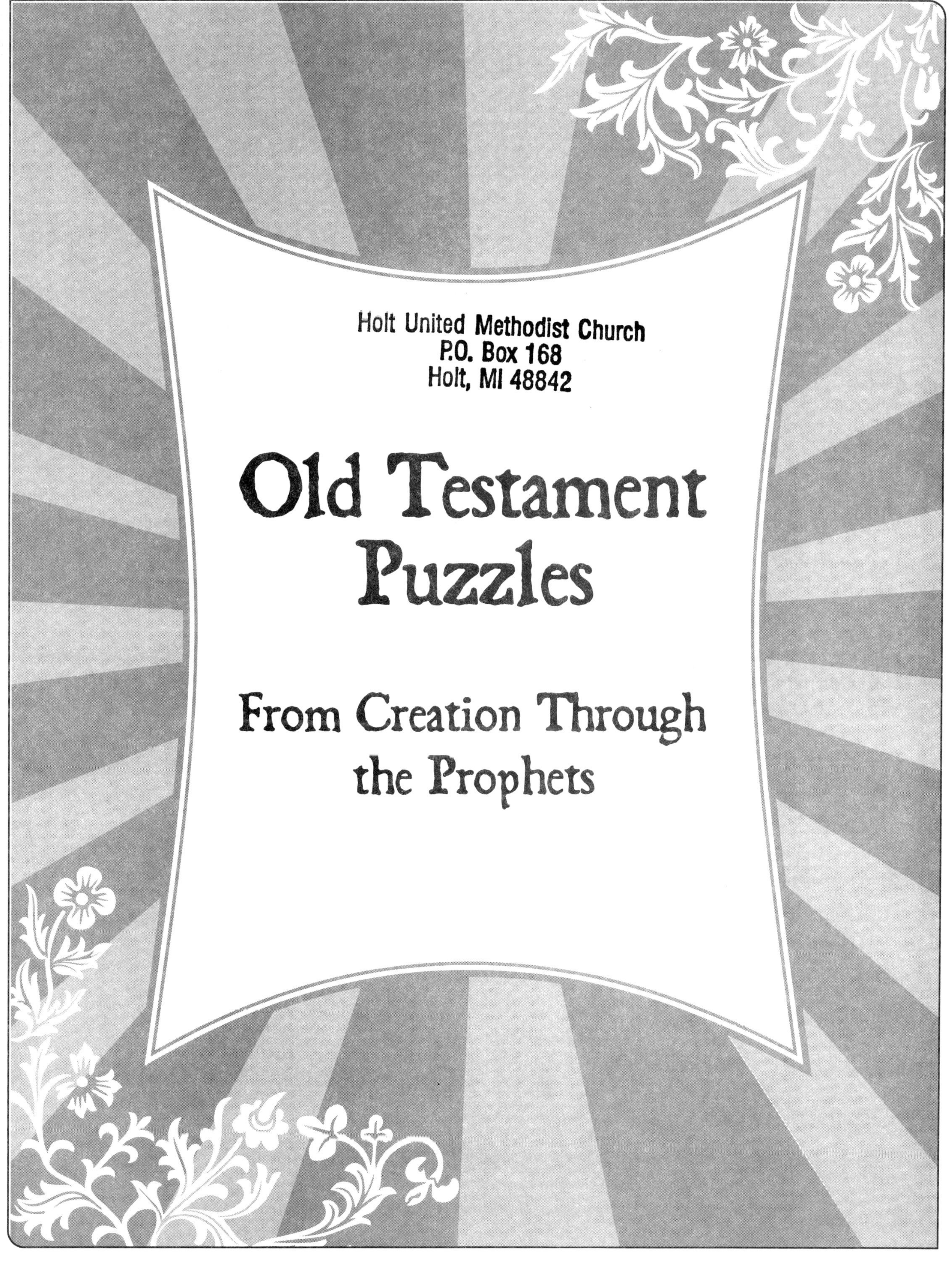

Old Testament Puzzles

From Creation Through the Prophets

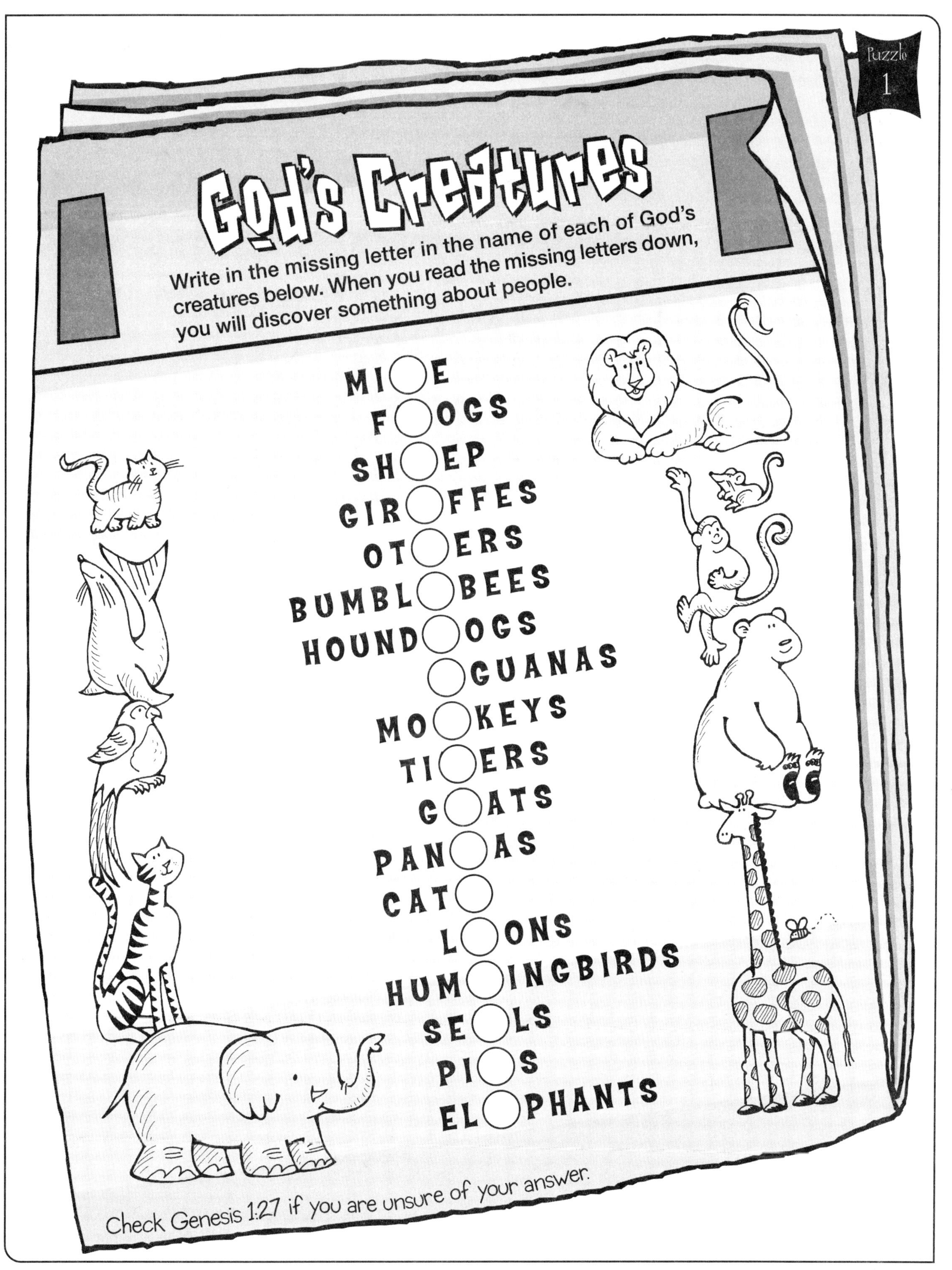

God's Creatures

Write in the missing letter in the name of each of God's creatures below. When you read the missing letters down, you will discover something about people.

Puzzle 1

MI◯E
F◯OGS
SH◯EP
GIR◯FFES
OT◯ERS
BUMBL◯BEES
HOUND◯OGS
◯GUANAS
MO◯KEYS
TI◯ERS
G◯ATS
PAN◯AS
CAT◯
L◯ONS
HUM◯INGBIRDS
SE◯LS
PI◯S
EL◯PHANTS

Check Genesis 1:27 if you are unsure of your answer.

COLOR ME IN

Color in all the person figures to discover an important group you are a part of.

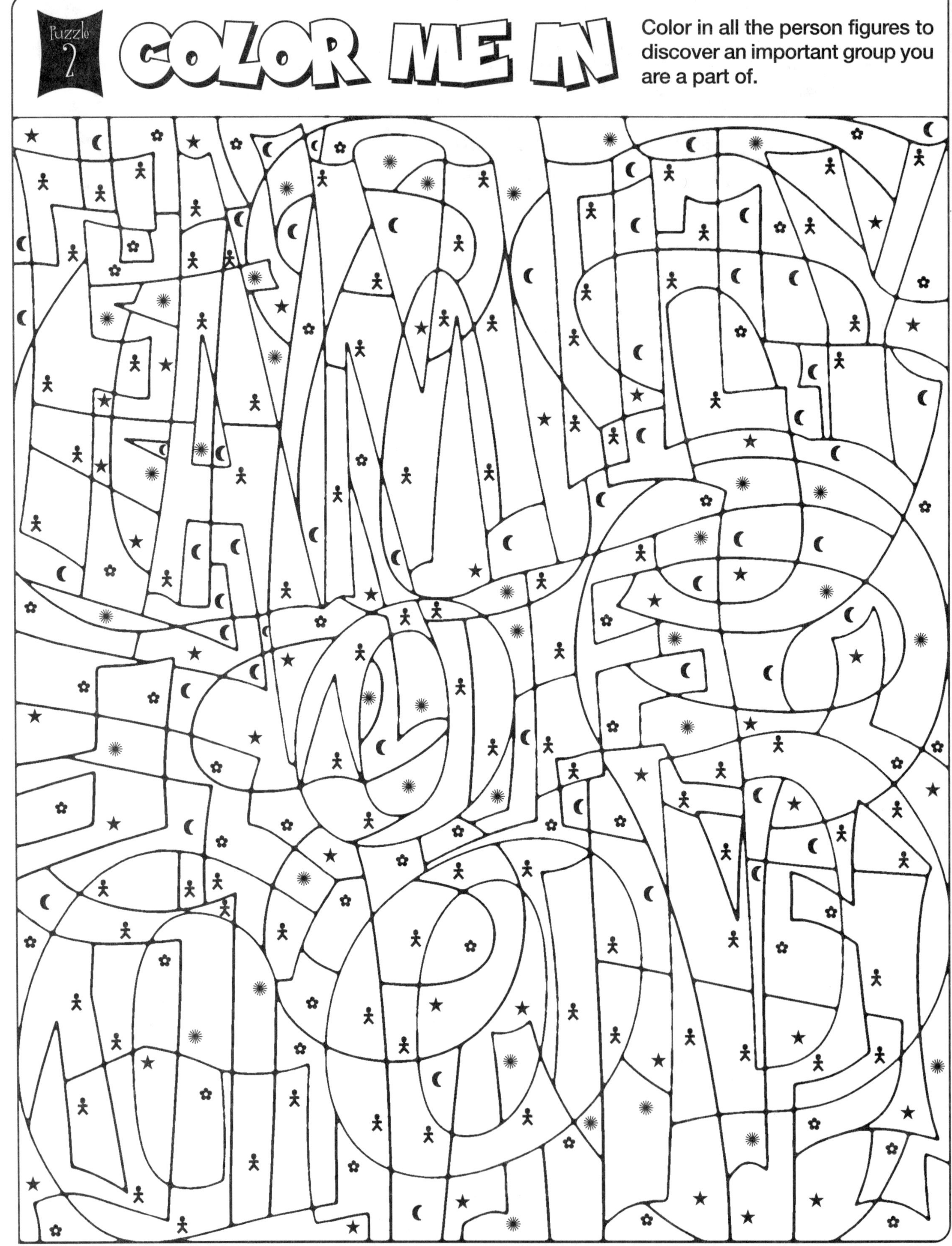

Letter to Letter

Begin at a lettered box and follow the line to an empty box.
Put that letter in the empty box. Keep following the lines
and filling in the letters until all the boxes are filled.

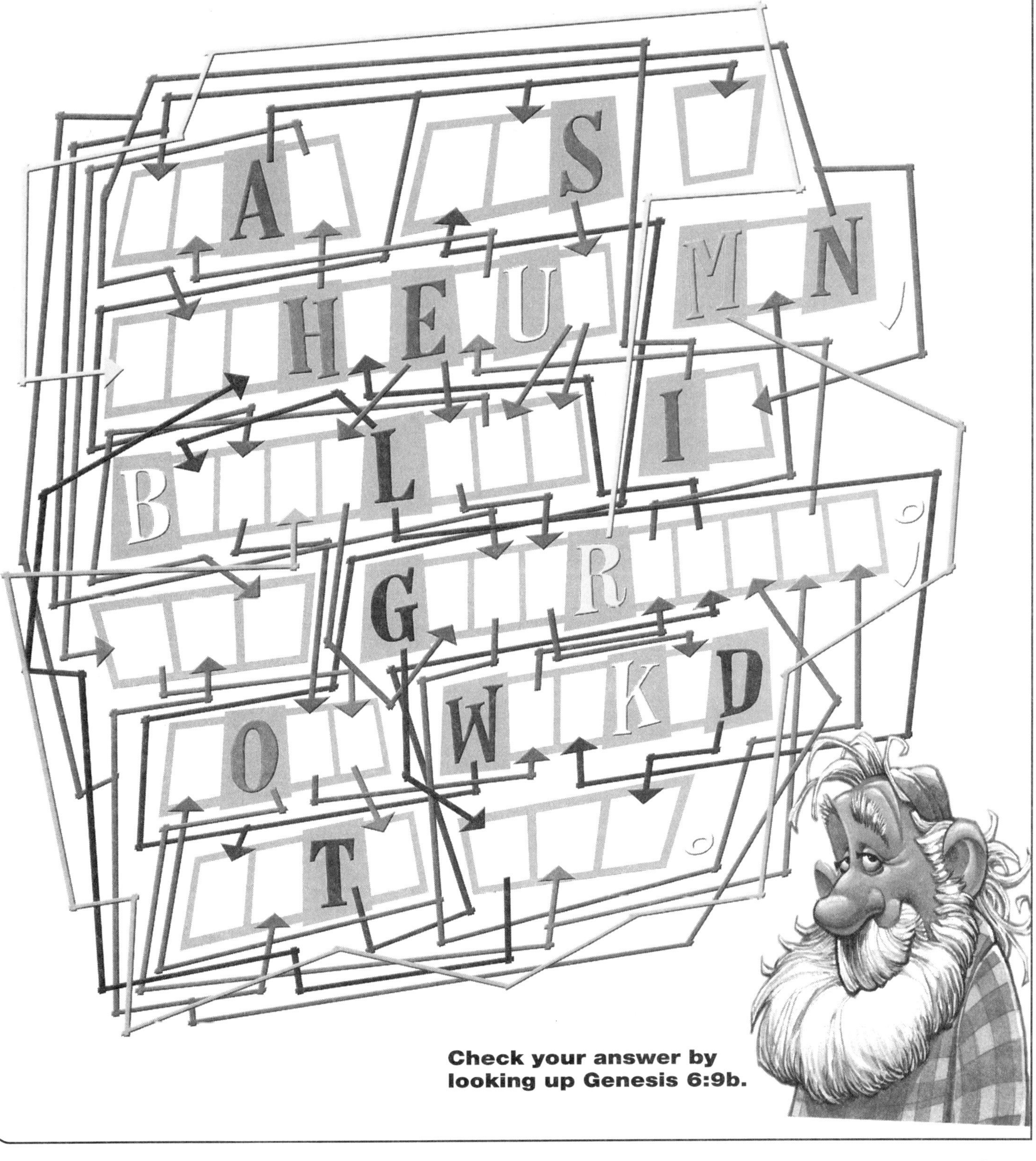

**Check your answer by
looking up Genesis 6:9b.**

HOW TO MAKE AN ARK

Choose the correct words and write them on the lines to complete God's instructions to Noah for making an ark.

This is how you are to make it:

 **Make yourself an ark of**

____.
(redwood, cypress wood, ebony)

 **Make**

____.
(rooms, bunk beds, stalls for the animals)

 **Cover it inside and out with**

____.
(shingles, pitch, a thatch roof)

 **Make the length**

____.
(sixteen feet, three miles, three hundred cubits)

 **Make the width**

____.
(fifty feet, five hundred feet, fifty cubits)

 **Make the height**

____.
(thirty feet, one mile, thirty cubits)

 **Make a**

____.
(roof, strong floor, large room divider)

 **Finish it to**

____.
(a cubit above, a cubit below, a cubit's overhang on each side)

 **Make the door of the ark**

____.
(at the front, at the back, in its side)

To finish your ark, decide how many decks it is to be.

____

Check Genesis 6:14-16.

   Old Testament Puzzles, © 2008 Abingdon Press

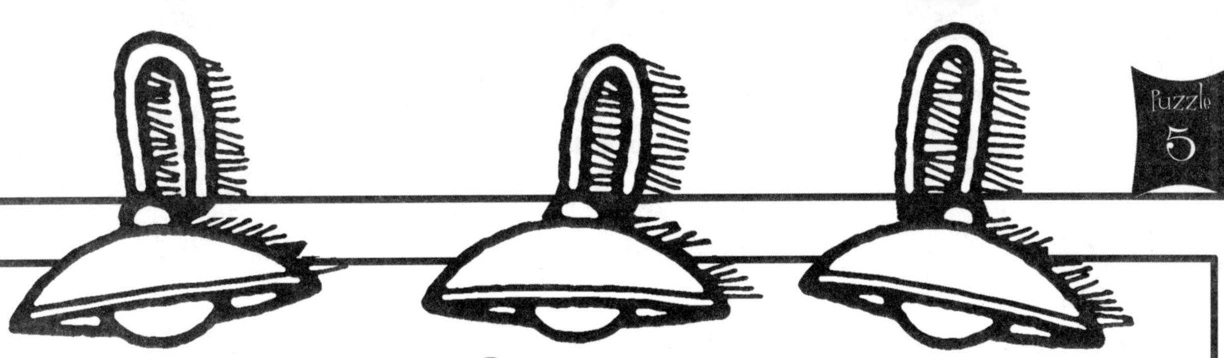

The Promise

Follow the directions to discover what God promised Abraham. Check your answer by reading Genesis 17:5c.

1. Moving left to right and line to line, cross out every **fourth** word.

2. Cross out all the pronouns except **YOU** and **I**.

3. Cross out all words that begin with **C**.

4. Cross out all **ten-letter** words.

5. Cross out all words that end in **Y**.

6. Cross out all words containing a **double vowel**.

we	they	I	state	count	certain	have
because	understand	made	you	advised	careful	noon
the	believe	fairly	ancestor	me	nephew	descendant
of	he	town	county	a	multitude	shall
donkey	of	him	countries	nearby	see	nations
forever	yesterday	clever	climb	nowhere	soon	certain

Decide whether each statement is true (T) or false (F). Draw lines connecting all the letters representing that statement's correct response. You will have a letter. Read down to complete: God said Abraham would be a _______________.

1. God told Abram that he would be the ancestor of a multitude of nations.

2. Abram's wife was Rebekah.

3. Abram's brother's son was Isaac.

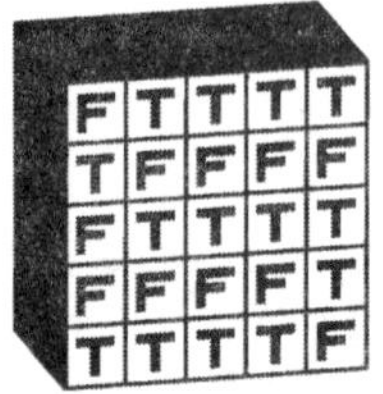

4. Sarai's name was changed to Sarah.

5. God made a covenant with Lot.

6. God appeared to Abraham when he was 76 years old.

7. God made a covenant with Abraham.

8. God told Abraham that he would have to move to Egypt.

Old Testament Puzzles, © 2008 Abingdon Press

BY THE SYLLABLE (sĭl'ə-bəl)

Puzzle 7

Fill in the lines for the words below using all the syllables in the box. In parentheses we have given you the number of syllables to be used for each word.

Mark out each syllable as you use it. For some words we have given you a hint. Check your answers by reading Psalm 105:8-9.

A	A	A	BRA	COM	COV	COV	E	E	ED	ER	ER	EV
FOR	FOR	FUL	GEN	HAM	HE	HE	HE	HIS	HIS	I	IS	ISE
MADE	MAND	MIND	NANT	NANT	OF	OF	PROM	SAAC	SAND			
SWORN	THAT	THAT	THE	THE	THOU	TIONS	TO	WITH	WORD			

1. (1) ___ ___ (pronoun)

2. (1) ___ ___ (means "to be")

3. (2) ___ ___ ___ ___

4. (1) ___ ___ (begins with the letter O)

5. (1) ___ ___ ___ (pronoun)

6. (3) ___ ___ ___ ___ ___ ___
(promise between God and people)

7. (3) ___ ___ ___ ___ ___ ___ (always),

8. (1) ___ ___ (same as number 4)

9. (1) ___ ___

10. (1) ___ ___ ___ (ends with D)

11. (1) ___ ___ ___ ___
(starts and ends with T)

12. (1) ___ ___

13. (3) ___ ___ ___ ___ ___ ___ ___,
(gave an order)

14. (1) ___ ___

15. (1) ___

16. (2) ___ ___ ___ ___ ___ ___
(a very large number)

17. (4) ___ ___ ___ ___ ___ ___ ___ ___ ___,
(parents, children, grandchildren)

18. (1) ___ ___

19. (3) ___ ___ ___ ___ ___ ___
(same word as number 6)

20. (1) ___ ___ ___

21. (1) ___ ___

22. (1) ___ ___

23. (1) ___ ___ ___ (together)

24. (3) ___ ___ ___ ___ ___ (name),

25. (1) ___ ___ ___ (pronoun)

26. (1) ___ ___

27. (2) ___ ___ ___ ___
(swear to do)

28. (1) ___ ___ (begins with T)

29. (2) ___ ___ ___ (son of 24).

Not Like the others

Each row below has one object that is different. Choose the letter from that object and write it in the box at the end of the row. Read down and you can complete the phrase:

God's promise is to every _________________________.

1. A C G O

2. S E F L

3. N E R I

4. A I E O

5. R S T P

6. A E I O

7. R S T P

8. A I E O

9. A E I O

10. Y S T N

Old Testament Puzzles, © 2008 Abingdon Press

SPIRAL MESSAGE

Mark out all of the Xs to unravel the maze and discover today's
Bible verse. Look up Philippians 4:11b to check your answer.

Jacob's Journey to God

Jacob was a complicated man. He was treacherous and capable of stealing. He even cheated his own twin and his father-in-law. In the end Jacob changed, became a righteous man, and turned to God. Can you trace Jacob's journey?

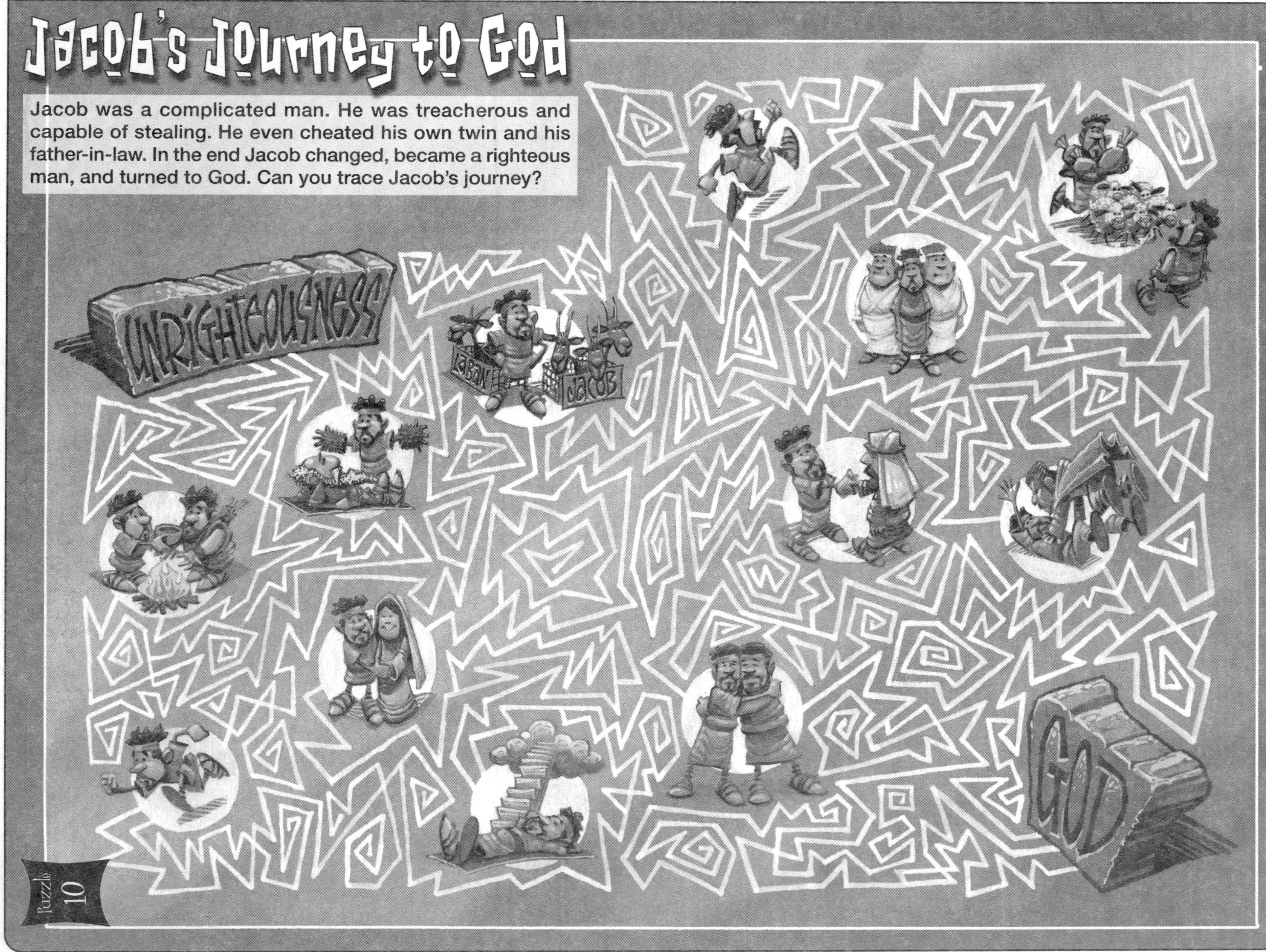

Old Testament Puzzles, © 2008 Abingdon Press

ANGRY WORD SEARCH

Joseph and his brothers had a lot of problems caused by anger. Find the words in the word search that show you what your life is filled with when you hold on to anger.

ANGER

HATRED

SIN

HURT

MALICE

BITTERNESS

JEALOUSY

SLANDER

GOSSIP

NAME THAT TRIBE!

THE twelve tribes of Israel are represented by the sons of Jacob. The tribe of Joseph was represented by two half-tribes because Jacob gave his favorite son a double portion of the land (Genesis 48:22). The half-tribes of Joseph were named for Joseph's two sons.

FIND the names of the twelve tribes of Israel in the faces of Jacob's sons and grandsons. Joseph got a double portion (Genesis 48:22). You may wish to use Genesis 35:23-26 and Genesis 48:20 for help with the hard names.

NOTE: Levi was not given land as one of the twelve tribes. Instead Levites were to be given places to live within the areas of the other tribes. (Numbers 34:1–35:8)

Change the Words

The Hebrew slaves had to work hard in Egypt, but God led them back to the Promised Land.

Can you go from *WORK* to *LAND* in four steps by changing only one letter in the word at each step?

As a young man, Moses killed an Egyptian. But later God called Moses to save the Hebrew slaves.

Can you go from *KILL* to *SAVE* in five steps?

Now try a harder one.

In the wilderness the Israelites needed something to drink. Moses had to find a place where there was water.

Go from *DRINK* to *PLACE* in five steps.

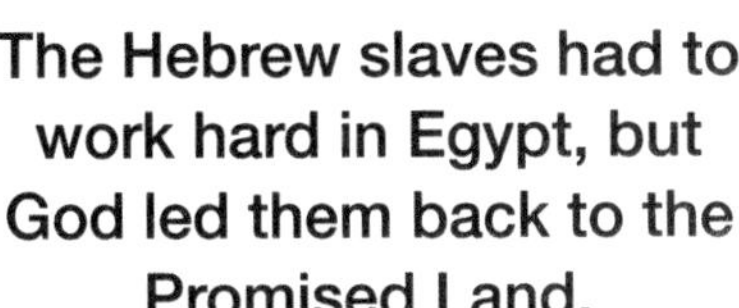

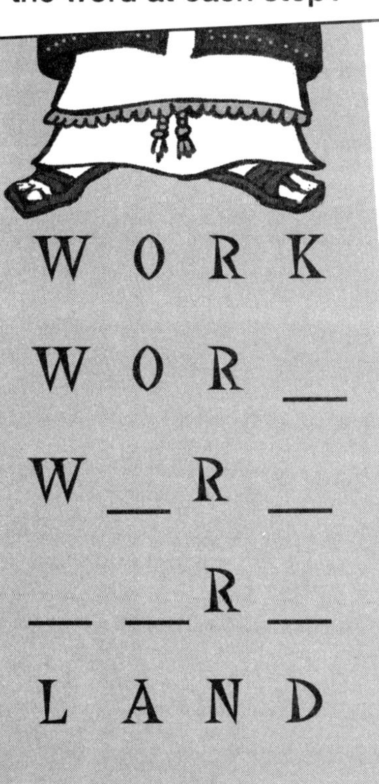

```
W O R K
W O R _
W _ R _
_ _ R _
L A N D
```

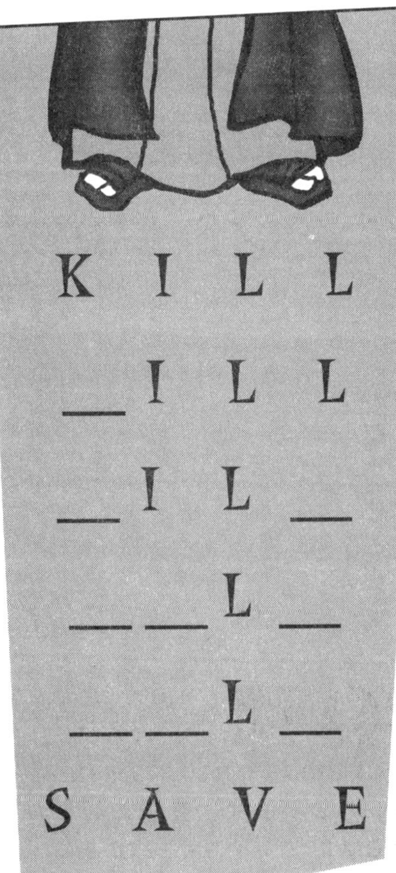

```
K I L L
_ I L L
_ I L _
_ _ L _
_ _ L _
S A V E
```

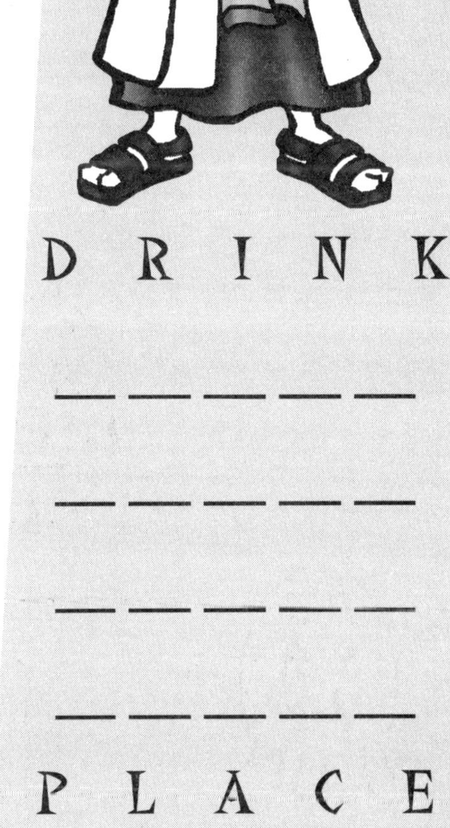

```
D R I N K
_ _ _ _ _
_ _ _ _ _
_ _ _ _ _
_ _ _ _ _
P L A C E
```

A PLACE FOR GOD

There was a holy place that God commanded Moses to construct. Follow the dots to find out what that place looked like.

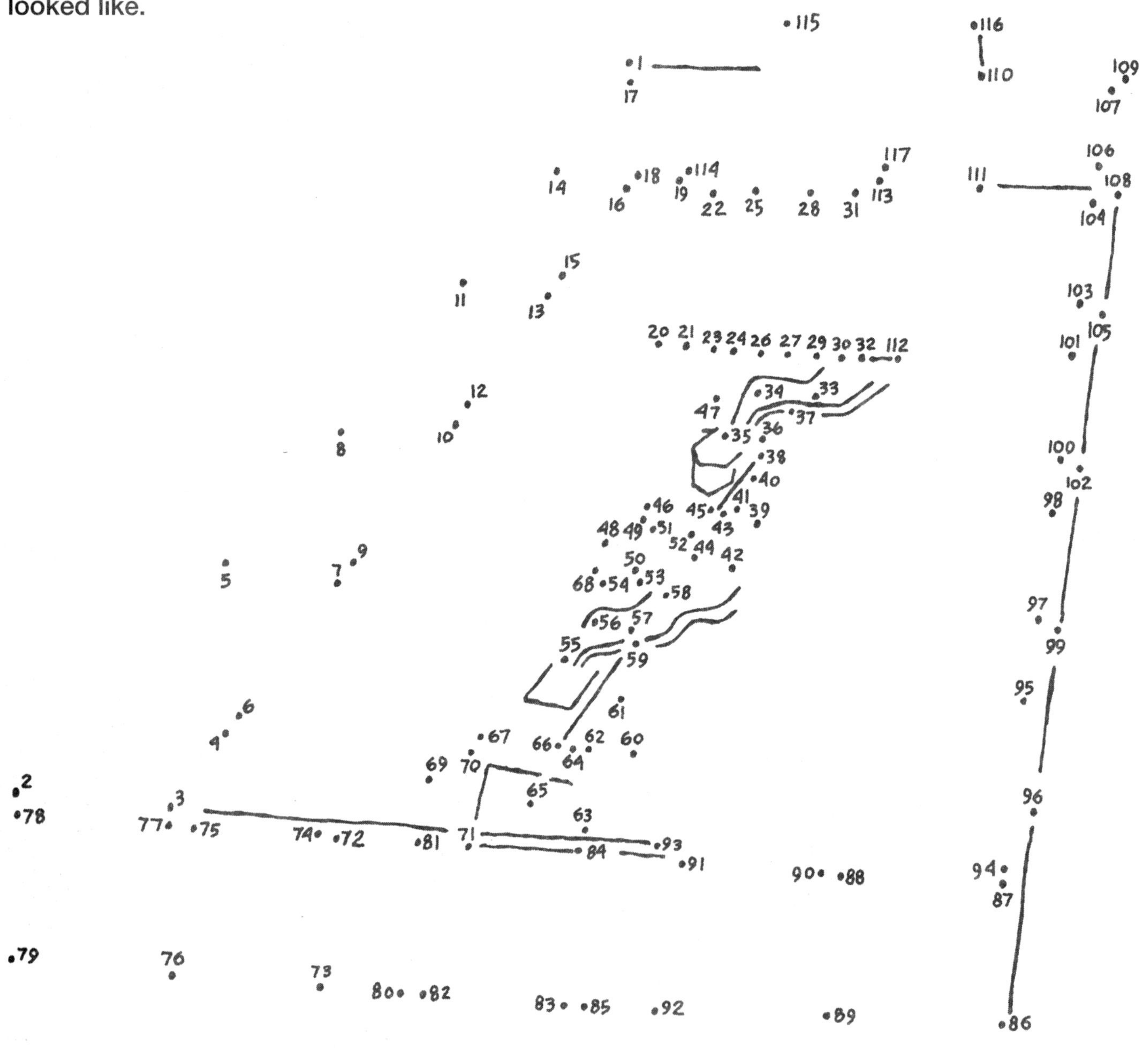

Old Testament Puzzles, © 2008 Abingdon Press

PICK 1

The words of the Bible verse are in order. But there's a catch. Some are in column A and some are in column B. Pick a word from either column A or column B and write it on the line below.

For example: The first word of the Bible verse is either **"Choose"** or **"Thanks."** Decide which word you think goes in the Bible verse below. Then continue down, choosing between column A and B.

A	B
CHOOSE	THANKS
YOUR	THIS
DAY	GOD
WHOM	THAT
THEY	YOU
HAVE	WILL
SERVE	BRING
BUT	NO
AS	TO
NEW	FOR
MY	ME
AND	FOR
MY	HE
COMPANION	HOUSEHOLD
YOU	WE
WILL	HAVE
SERVE	GIVEN
THE	SHE
GOLD	LORD

____

_____________ , . . . _______________,

_______________________________________.

Check Joshua 24:15b and 24:15d. (We left out part of the Scripture. It's a long one!)

DECODE IT

Decode the puzzle below to discover something about our relationship with God. Check your answer by reading Joshua 1:9.

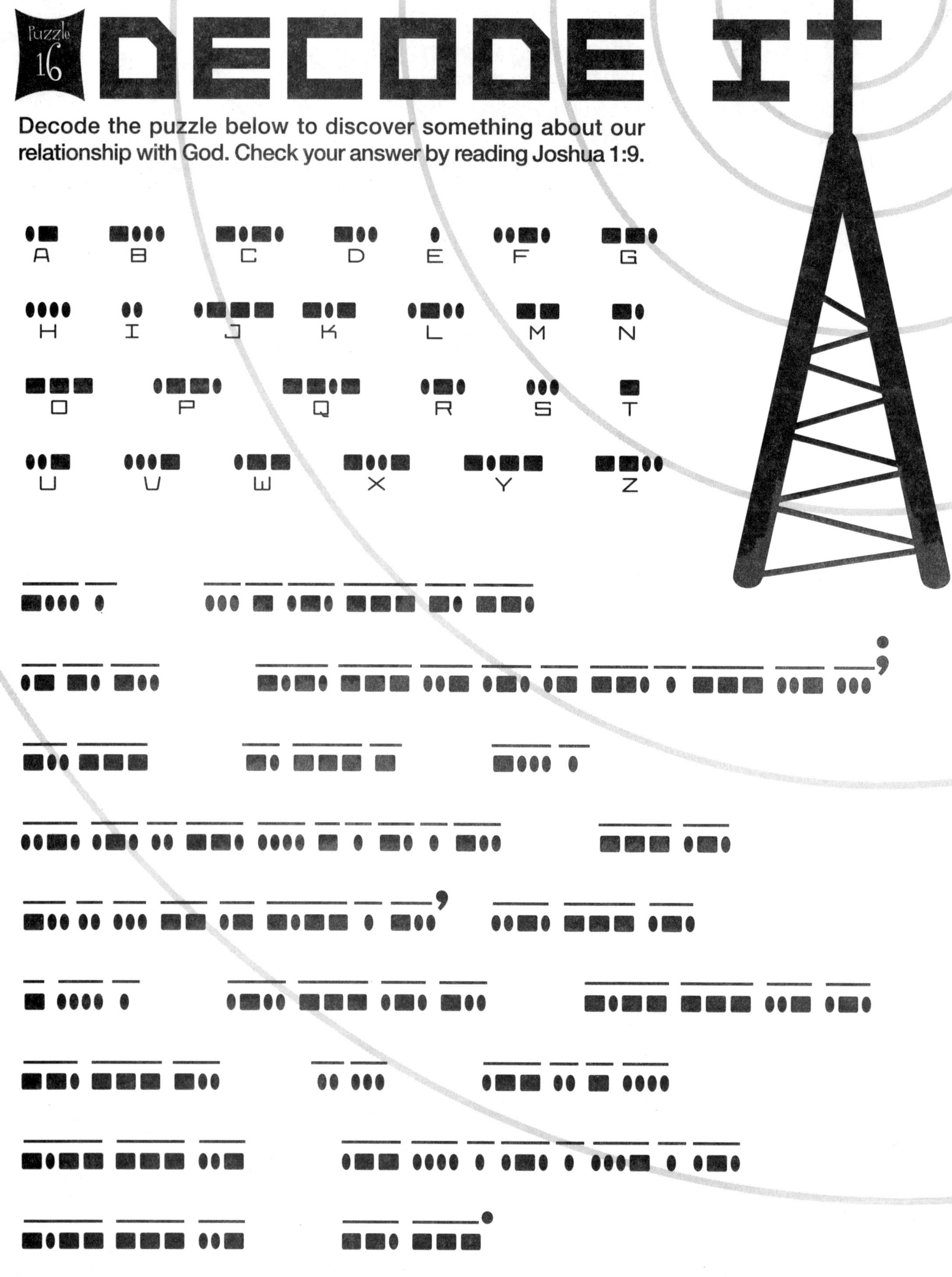

Old Testament Puzzles, © 2008 Abingdon Press

LETTER CLUES

Use the clues to help you fill in the blanks below to discover today's Bible verse.

Hint #1—Write down the alphabet. Write down each letter of the alphabet the number of times the clues tell you. Mark them off as they are used. Mark off any letter of the alphabet the clues tell you are not used.

Clue #1—The letters *B, C, J, M, Q, X, Y,* and *Z* are not used at all.

Clue #2—The letters *D, I, F, U,* and *V* are used only 1 time each.

Clue #3—The letters *A, K, N,* and *P* are used 2 times each.

Clue #4—The vowel *O* is used 9 times! The tenth word ends in *O*. This word is often used at the beginning of a question.

Clue #5—The letters *G, L,* and *S* are each used 3 times. Word 4 ends in 2 *L*s.

Clue #6—The letters *R* and *W* are each used 4 times.

Clue #7—The letter *H* is used 5 times, while the letters *E* and *T* are both used 6 times.

Clue #8—Word 11 means the opposite of *HATE*.

Clue #9—Words 8, 9, and 12 all have an *O* exactly in the middle of the word. Words 6 & 7 have *O* as the second letter in the word.

Clue #10—Word 3 begins in *T* and ends in *T*. Words 5, 7, and 9 all begin with *T*.

Clue #11—Word 2 begins with *K* while word 6 ends with a *K*.

Clue #12—Both *P*s are in word 13 (the last word)—letters number 1 and 4. This is the word that uses the only *U*. The *U* comes after one of the *P*s.

Clue #13—Word 4 begins with *A*.

Clue #14—In word 7 the third letter is *G* and the sixth letter is *H*.

Clue #15—*E* is the last letter of words 1, 9, 11, and 13.

Clue #16—Word 5 ends in *GS*.

Clue #17—Word 8 begins with *F* and word 12 begins with *G*.

Clue #18—There are two *E*s in word 7.

Clue #19—Words 1, 6, and 10 all begin with *W* while word 2 ends in *W*.

Clue #20—Look up the verse in the Bible.

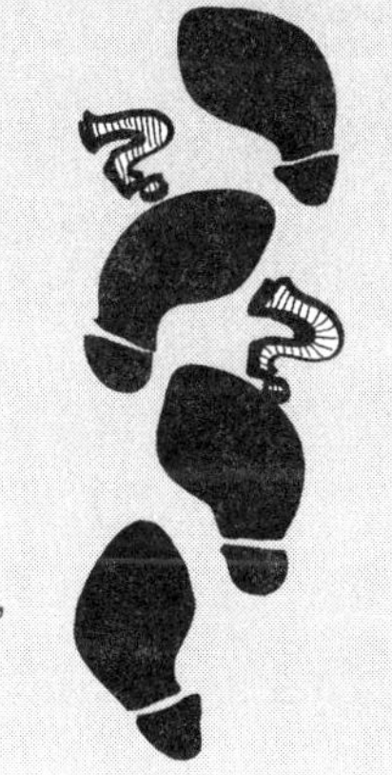

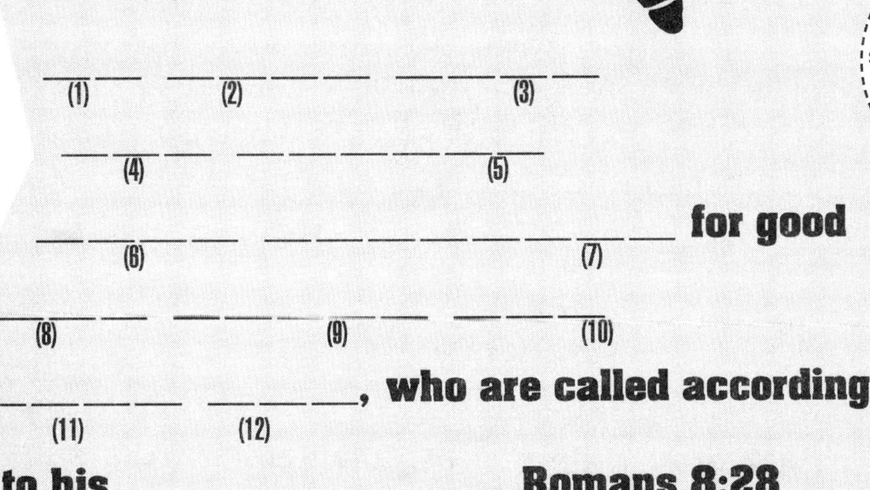

(1) _______ (2) _______ (3) _______

(4) _______ (5) _______

(6) _______ (7) _______ **for good**

(8) _______ (9) _______ (10) _______

(11) _______ (12) _______, **who are called according**

to his (13) _______. **Romans 8:28**

WHICH LETTERS?

Find one letter in each group that every word in that group of words has in common. Write that letter in the circle. Unscramble the letters and write them in the circles below to discover an important phrase from the Song of Deborah. To check your answer read Judges 5:2.

JUDE   EXODUS   SUNDAY   DANIEL   JUDGES 

JOHN   DEUTERONOMY   HOSEA   AMOS   TIMOTHY 

LUKE   THESSALONIANS   GALATIANS   CHRONICLES   EZEKIEL 

GENESIS   PHILEMON   PETER   HEBREWS   LOVE 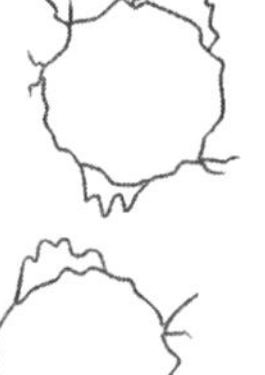

PSALMS   TITUS   ACTS   SAMUEL   JOSHUA 

ESTHER   JAMES   THESSALONIANS   ROMANS   ECCLESIASTES 

HABAKKUK   OBADIAH   PROVERBS   BIBLE   JOB 

REVELATION   CHRONICLES   GALATIANS   SAMUEL   PHILEMON 

MARK   HEBREWS   PROVERBS   ZECHARIAH   RUTH 

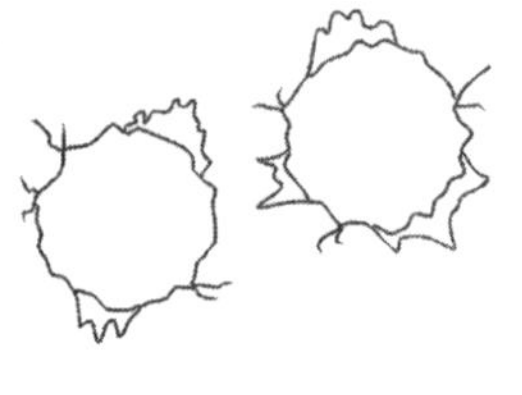 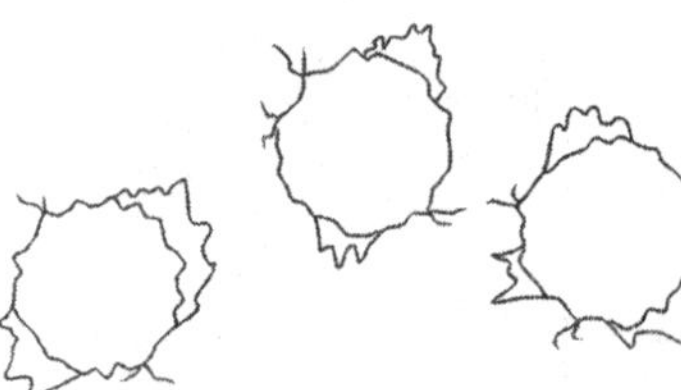  THE 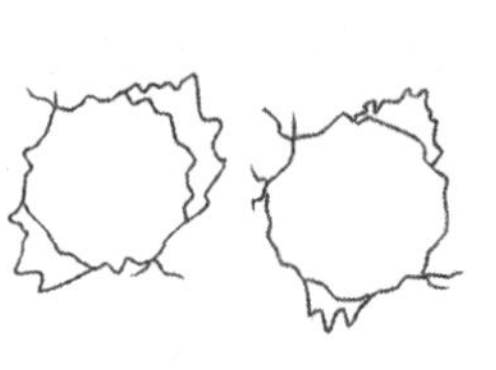  

Dropped Out

Letters have been dropped out of the alphabet. Write the missing letter from each alphabet on the line. Then read down the lines to discover what Psalm 47:8 says.

ABCDEFHIJKLMNOPQRSTUVWXYZ	___	ABCDEFHIJKLMNOPQRSTUVWXYZ	___
ABCDEFGHIJKLMNPQRSTUVWXYZ	___	ABCDEFGHIJKLMNPQRSTUVWXYZ	___
ABCEFGHIJKLMNOPQRSTUVWXYZ	___	ABCEFGHIJKLMNOPQRSTUVWXYZ	___
ABCDEFGHJKLMNOPQRSTUVWXYZ	___	ABCDEFGHIJKLMNOPQRTUVWXYZ	___
ABCDEFGHIJKLMNOPQRTUVWXYZ	___	ABCDEFGHJKLMNOPQRSTUVWXYZ	___
ABCDEFGHIJLMNOPQRSTUVWXYZ	___	ABCDEFGHIJKLMNOPQRSUVWXYZ	___
ABCDEFGHJKLMNOPQRSTUVWXYZ	___	ABCDEFGHIJKLMNOPQRTUVWXYZ	___
ABCDEFGHIJKLMOPQRSTUVWXYZ	___	ABCDEFGHIJKLMNPQRSTUVWXYZ	___
ABCDEFHIJKLMNOPQRSTUVWXYZ	___	ABCDEFGHIJKLMOPQRSTUVWXYZ	___
ABCDEFGHIJKLMNPQRSTUVWXYZ	___	ABCDEFGIJKLMNOPQRSTUVWXYZ	___
ABCDEFGHIJKLMNOPQRSTUWXYZ	___	ABCDEFGHJKLMNOPQRSTUVWXYZ	___
ABCDFGHIJKLMNOPQRSTUVWXYZ	___	ABCDEFGHIJKLMNOPQRTUVWXYZ	___
ABCDEFGHIJKLMNOPQSTUVWXYZ	___	ABCDEFGIJKLMNOPQRSTUVWXYZ	___
ABCDEFGHIJKLMNOPQRSUVWXYZ	___	ABCDEFGHIJKLMNPQRSTUVWXYZ	___
ABCDEFGIJKLMNOPQRSTUVWXYZ	___	ABCDEFGHIJKMNOPQRSTUVWXYZ	___
ABCDFGHIJKLMNOPQRSTUVWXYZ	___	ABCDEFGHIJKLMNOPQRSTUVWXZ	___
ABCDEFGHIJKLMOPQRSTUVWXYZ	___	ABCDEFGHIJKLMNOPQRSUVWXYZ	___
BCDEFGHIJKLMNOPQRSTUVWXYZ	___	ABCDEFGIJKLMNOPQRSTUVWXYZ	___
ABCDEFGHIJKLMNOPQRSUVWXYZ	___	ABCDEFGHIJKLMNOPQSTUVWXYZ	___
ABCDEFGHIJKLMNOPQRSTUVWXYZ	___	ABCDEFGHIJKLMNPQRSTUVWXYZ	___
ABCDEFGHIJKLMNPQRSTUVWXYZ	___	ABCDEFGHIJKLMOPQRSTUVWXYZ	___
ABCDEFGHIJKLMOPQRSTUVWXYZ	___	ABCDFGHIJKLMNOPQRSTUVWXYZ	___
ABCDEFGHIJKLMNOPQRTUVWXYZ	___		

Saul's Story

Below is the story of Saul. See if you can put it in order. The Bible references would give the answers away, so just take your best shot.

____ Saul gets tired of waiting for Samuel and makes an unlawful sacrifice. (This is Samuel's job.)

____ Saul becomes jealous of David.

____ The people of Israel demand a king.

____ A young boy, David, plays the lyre to soothe Saul.

____ Saul fights battles and defeats the Ammonites.

____ God tells the judge and prophet Samuel to give the people a king.

____ David spares Saul's life.

____ Saul begins to turn from God.

____ Saul's three sons are killed in battle and Saul falls on his own sword.

____ Saul is tormented because the Spirit of the Lord has departed from him.

____ A handsome young man named Saul visits Samuel. The Lord reveals to Samuel that Saul should be king.

____ David kills Goliath and becomes a great warrior.

____ Saul tries to kill David.

____ Samuel anoints Saul king.

Can You Do It?

Fill in the blanks with the words scattered around the page to discover the way God wants us to live. Check your answer in 1 Kings 2:2b–3b.

courageous

ways

statutes

STRONG

CHARGE

keeping

ordinances

commandments

keep

walking

testimonies

Be ________________, be ________________, and ________________ the

________________ of the LORD your God, ________________ in his ________________

and ________________ his ________________, his

________________, his ________________, and his

________________.

David's Connections

What are the names of these people connected to King David? Write the name on the line provided. Be careful! Two of these people have no immediate connection to David. Just put an *X* through the lines connecting these two people to David.

helped bring peace
(1 Samuel 25:18)

known as the great lawgiver
(Exodus 19:25–20:17)

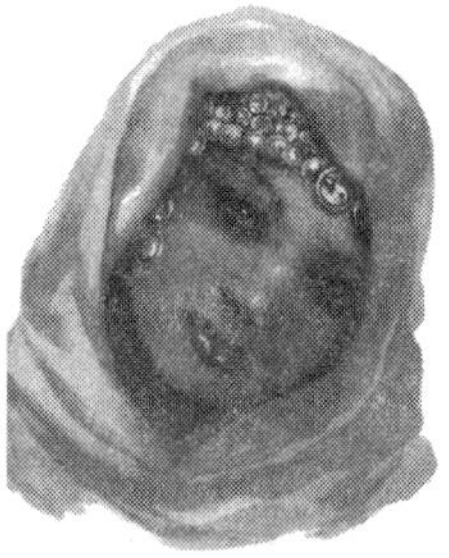

mother of Solomon
(2 Samuel 12:24)

good friend
(1 Samuel 20:16)

DAVID

judge
(Judges 4–5)

judge who anointed kings
(1 Samuel 16:13)

first king of Israel
(1 Samuel 9:22–10:1)

third king of Israel
(1 Kings 1:38-40)

prophet
(2 Samuel 12:1)

Old Testament Puzzles, © 2008 Abingdon Press

CHANGE THE LETTERS

Follow the directions to solve the code and discover where to turn during rough times.

C J K M Q J X S S B Z X C B

N T K Q D S B T C D Y N

L B S I V S B Q B T D

Y B P V M T D S J X F P B .

(PSALM 46:1)

1. Change the letter *S* to *R*.
2. Change the letter *Q* to *S*.
3. Change the letter *J* to *O*.
4. Change the letter *Y* to *H*.
5. Change the letter *B* to *E*.
6. Change the letter *N* to *A*.
7. Change the letter *T* to *N*.
8. Change the letter *V* to *P*.
9. Change the letter *P* to *L*.
10. Change the letter *Z* to *F*.
11. Change the letter *F* to *B*.
12. Change the letter *D* to *T*.
13. Change the letter *X* to *U*.
14. Change the letter *L* to *V*.
15. Change the letter *M* to *I*.
15. Change the letter *K* to *D*.
17. Change the letter *C* to *G*.
18. Change the letter *I* to *Y*.

A Prayer From the Psalms

A word is hidden in each line of letters. Find each word and write it on the lines below (in order found). You will discover part of a prayer that comes from the Psalms. The answer is found in Psalm 119:34. (We've put the "I" in the puzzle for you.)

```
A B B C W G I V E D O Y L T S M G V O
M D O L A N T Y G M S U G I M E S V U
W U N D E R S T A N D I N G L T A E T
T H A T M W N E O S C P R I V U D T L
X Z Y A B C M A Y K E E G L I V X U M
K E E G Y O K E E P N U V Z T S E G
Y N D E A S T E R D Y O U R L A C L
L A W X N N E S O A G M L Y T E D S
A P Z A P L A R O A N D A P Z X D Y A
O L N Y O B S E R V E O D G E V S T
I T N O V W M C C C D A E I O U Y V
W M N P Q R A B C D W I T H V I X E
M O T D H S P R I N M Y L S Y M N P O
U V Y W X Z J F P D C B A W H O L E
N E A B C D E F G H E A R T I J K L M
```

_____ __ ____________,

____ I ___ ____ ____

__ _______ __ _____ _____.

     Old Testament Puzzles, © 2008 Abingdon Press

A PROMISE TO THE FAMILY OF GOD

Through Jeremiah, God made a promise. To discover it, fill in the blanks below with the secret message. Begin with the first vertical row. Go from top to bottom, copying down the letters you find to the left of the dots. Do the same for each row, moving from the bottom of one row to the top of the next. The letters are in order in the message. Check your answer in Jeremiah 23:5b.

IT'S BACKWARD!

THE DAYS
ARE SURELY COMING SAYS
THE LORD WHEN I WILL RAISE
UP FOR DAVID A RIGHTEOUS
BRANCH AND HE SHALL REIGN
AS KING AND DEAL WISELY AND
SHALL EXECUTE JUSTICE AND
RIGHTEOUSNESS IN THE LAND

By the way, there are no spaces between the words and there is no punctuation!

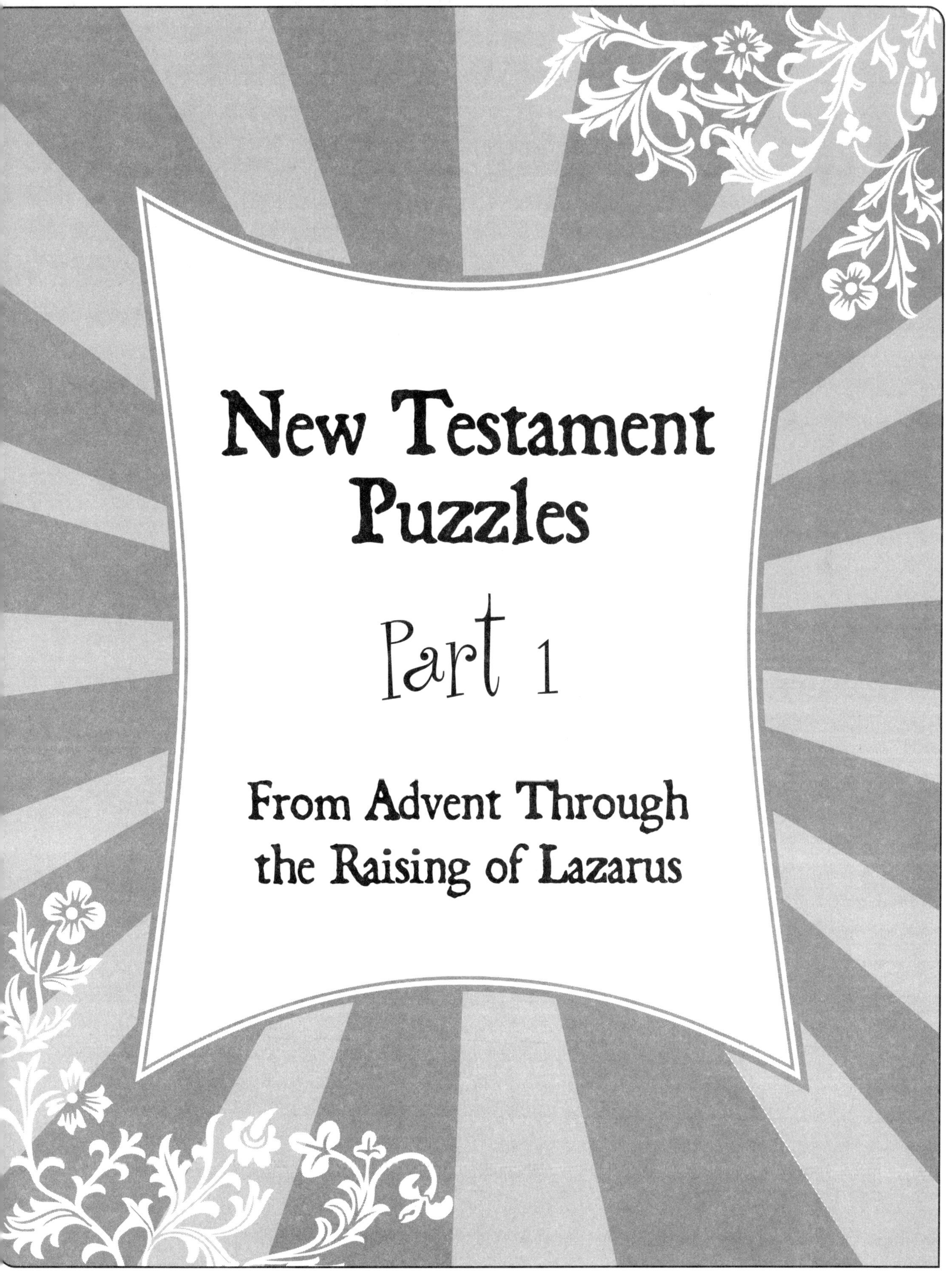

New Testament Puzzles
Part 1
From Advent Through
the Raising of Lazarus

Jesus' Ancestry

For the first readers of the Book of Matthew, it was important to know the ancestors of Jesus. You will find their names in the first chapter. Use your Bibles to fill in their names. Each letter in the words below will be the first letter in the name of one of the ancestors found in the first chapter. You may use some names twice, but not in the same word. (*Tamar* has already been filled in for you.)

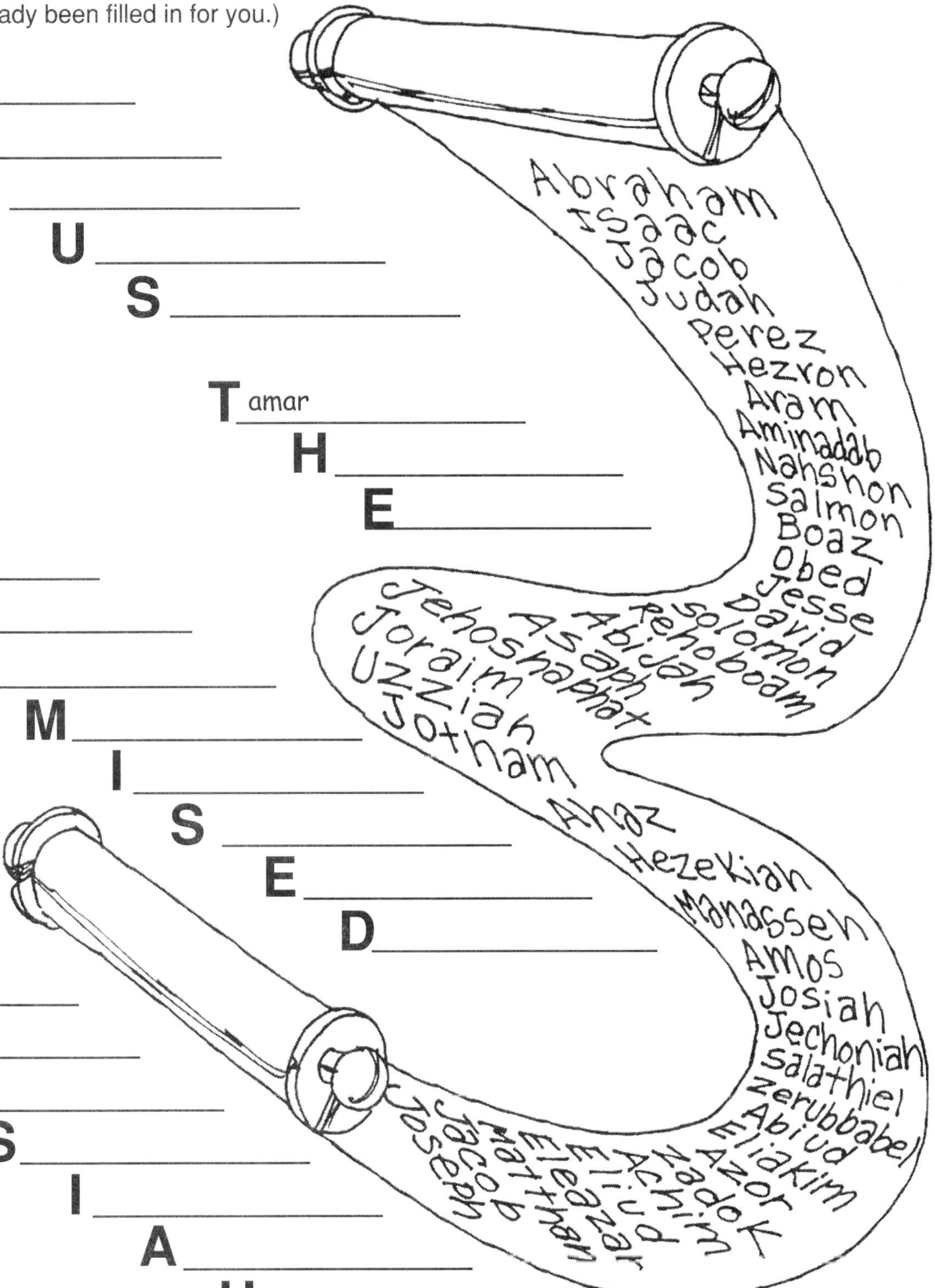

J _______________
  E _______________
    S _______________
      U _______________
        S _______________

          T *amar* _______________
            H _______________
              E _______________

P _______________
  R _______________
    O _______________
      M _______________
        I _______________
          S _______________
            E _______________
              D _______________

M _______________
  E _______________
    S _______________
      S _______________
        I _______________
          A _______________
            H _______________

STORY BY THE NUMBERS

1. God promised to make him the ancestor of a great nation. BRMHAAA __ __ ◯ __ __ __ __

2. Wife of 1. ASHAR __ __ ◯ __ __

3. The promised son of 1 & 2. ASAIC ◯ __ __ __ __ __

4. Youngest son of 3. His name was changed by God from *Jacob* to LEARIS __ __ __ __ ◯ __ .

5. Son of 3. Twin brother of 4. He sold his birthright to 4. UEAS ◯ __ __ __

6. Favorite son of 4. He was sold by his brothers into Egypt. SHOJPE __ ◯ __ __ __ __

7. After 6 moved his family to Egypt, the Hebrews became slaves. After a long time they were freed from slavery by SEMOS __ __ __ ◯ __ .

8. After 7 died, the Israelites needed a new leader. They were led into the Promised Land by HUJOSA __ __ __ __ __ ◯ .

9. After 8 died, the Israelites needed leaders (called judges) when they got in trouble. One of those leaders was a woman named BODERHA __ ◯ __ __ __ __ __ .

10. Soon the Israelites didn't want people like 9 to lead them. They demanded a ruler like those of other nations. Soon they had a new leader, NIGK LAUS __ __ __ ◯ __ __ __ __ .

11. After the death of 10, he became king. VIDDA __ __ ◯ __ __

12. After 10 and 11, he became king of all Israel. MOOONSL __ __ __ __ __ __ __ ◯

13. 10 was the first king, but only 11 and 12 ruled a united country. After the death of 12, the country became a VIDDEDI GMIDKON. __ __ __ __ __ __ __ __ __ __ ◯ __ __ __ .

14. The kings of 13 kept straying from the Lord, so God raised up these people to advise the kings. ORPHEPST __ __ __ __ __ __ ◯ __

15. As 13 fell, 14 told of a new king, a Messiah to come from the line of 11 who would come to save the people. The Messiah's earthly mother was YARM __ __ __ ◯ .

Unscramble the circled letters to complete the message below.

The Messiah brought a renewed promise of salvation to

__ __ __ __ __ __   __ __ __ __ __ __ __ __ __ __ __ __ .

Puzzle 29

Mary's Song

Mary's Song is in all versions of the Bible in Luke 1:46-56. The words are slightly different, but all express Mary's heartfelt praise to God. Below are some verses from the King James Version (KJV). Using a New Revised Standard Version (NRSV), locate each verse and find the synonym (a word that means the same) for each underlined word or words. Write these words on the lines. Then rearrange the letters in the music notes to form a Latin name for Mary's Song.

And Mary said, My soul <u>doth magnify</u> the Lord.

For he hath regarded the low estate of his <u>handmaiden</u>.

From <u>henceforth</u> all generations shall call me blessed.

He hath scattered the proud in the <u>imagination</u> of their hearts.

He hath put down the mighty from their <u>seats</u>.

As he spake to our <u>fathers</u>, to Abraham, and

to his <u>seed</u> for ever.

And Mary <u>abode</u> with her [Elizabeth] about three months.

In Latin, Mary's Song is known as the

WHO PROPHESIED THAT?

The prophets of the Old Testament made predictions about the Messiah. Draw lines matching the Old Testament prophecy with the New Testament Scripture and the event predicted.

Jeremiah 26:5

Matthew 23:15

MESSIAH WILL BE DAVID'S DESCENDANT

THE MESSIAH WILL RETURN FROM EGYPT

John 7:40-43

Hosea 11:1

Isaiah 7:14

Luke 2:11

THE MESSIAH WILL BE A RESIDENT OF BETHLEHEM

Matthew 1:21-23

THE MESSIAH WILL BE BORN OF A VIRGIN

Micah 5:2

New Testament Puzzles (1), © 2008 Abingdon Press

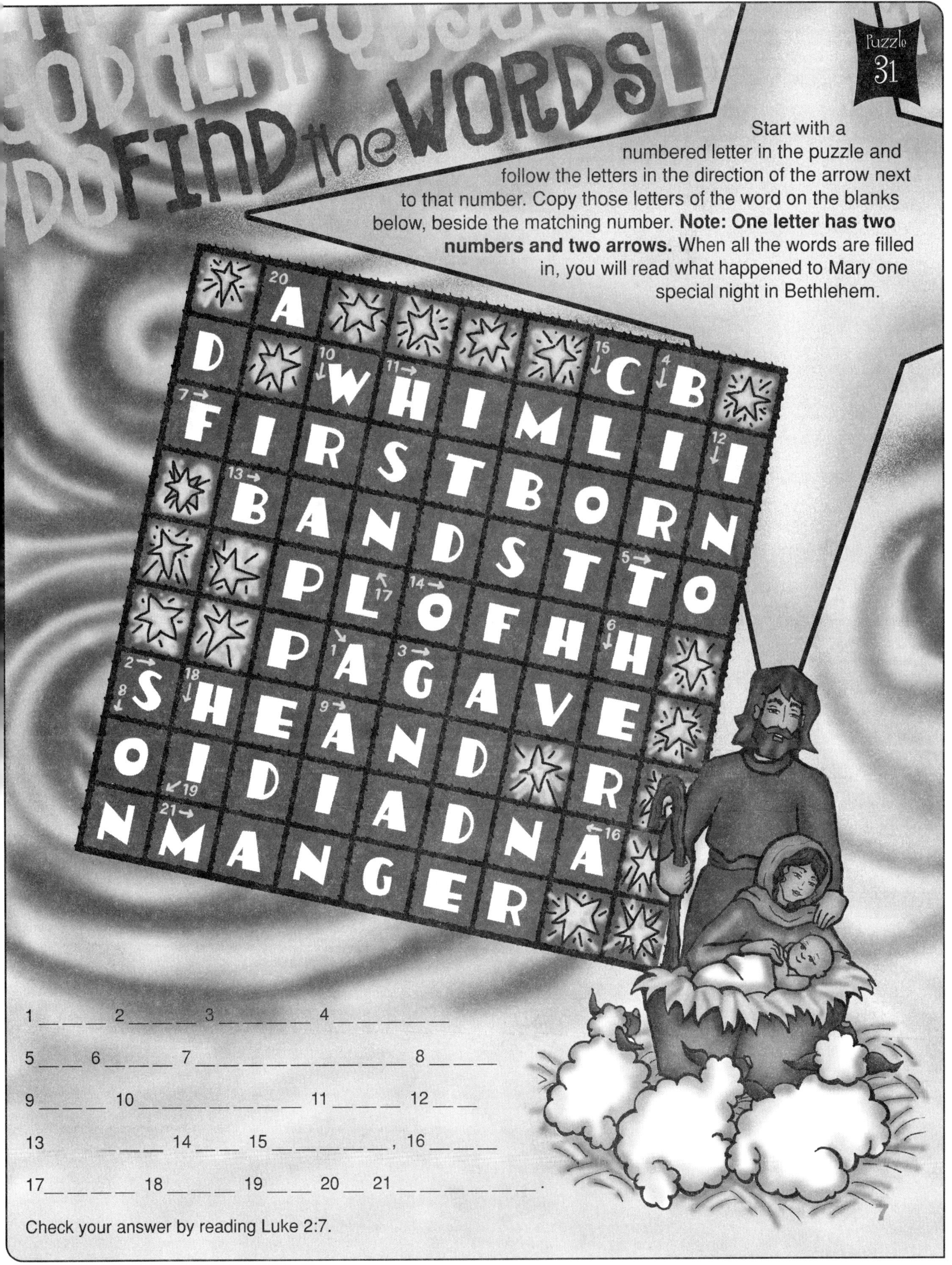

Start with a numbered letter in the puzzle and follow the letters in the direction of the arrow next to that number. Copy those letters of the word on the blanks below, beside the matching number. **Note: One letter has two numbers and two arrows.** When all the words are filled in, you will read what happened to Mary one special night in Bethlehem.

1 __ __ __ __   2 __ __ __   3 __ __ __   4 __ __ __ __ __

5 __ __   6 __ __ __   7 __ __ __ __ __ __ __   8 __ __ __

9 __ __ __   10 __ __ __ __   11 __ __ __   12 __ __

13 __ __ __   14 __ __   15 __ __ __ __ , 16 __ __ __

17 __ __ __   18 __ __ __   19 __ __   20 __   21 __ __ __ __ __

Check your answer by reading Luke 2:7.

Use the two word lists to fill in the grid. The words are from the Bible story found in Luke 2:1-5, but one of the words does not belong. Which word is it? Why is this word not found in this Scripture?

Clueless Crossword

HINT: Start with the word that stretches between the *Q* and the *S* on the grid.

VERTICAL:
ALSO, ANGRILY, AUGUSTUS, BECAUSE, CALLED, CHILD, DECREE, DESCENDED, EXPECTING, FAMILY, FIRST, FROM, GALILEE, GOVERNOR, HE, HOUSE, NAZARETH, OF, THE, THEIR, THIS, TO, TOWN, WENT, WHILE, WHO, WHOM, WORLD

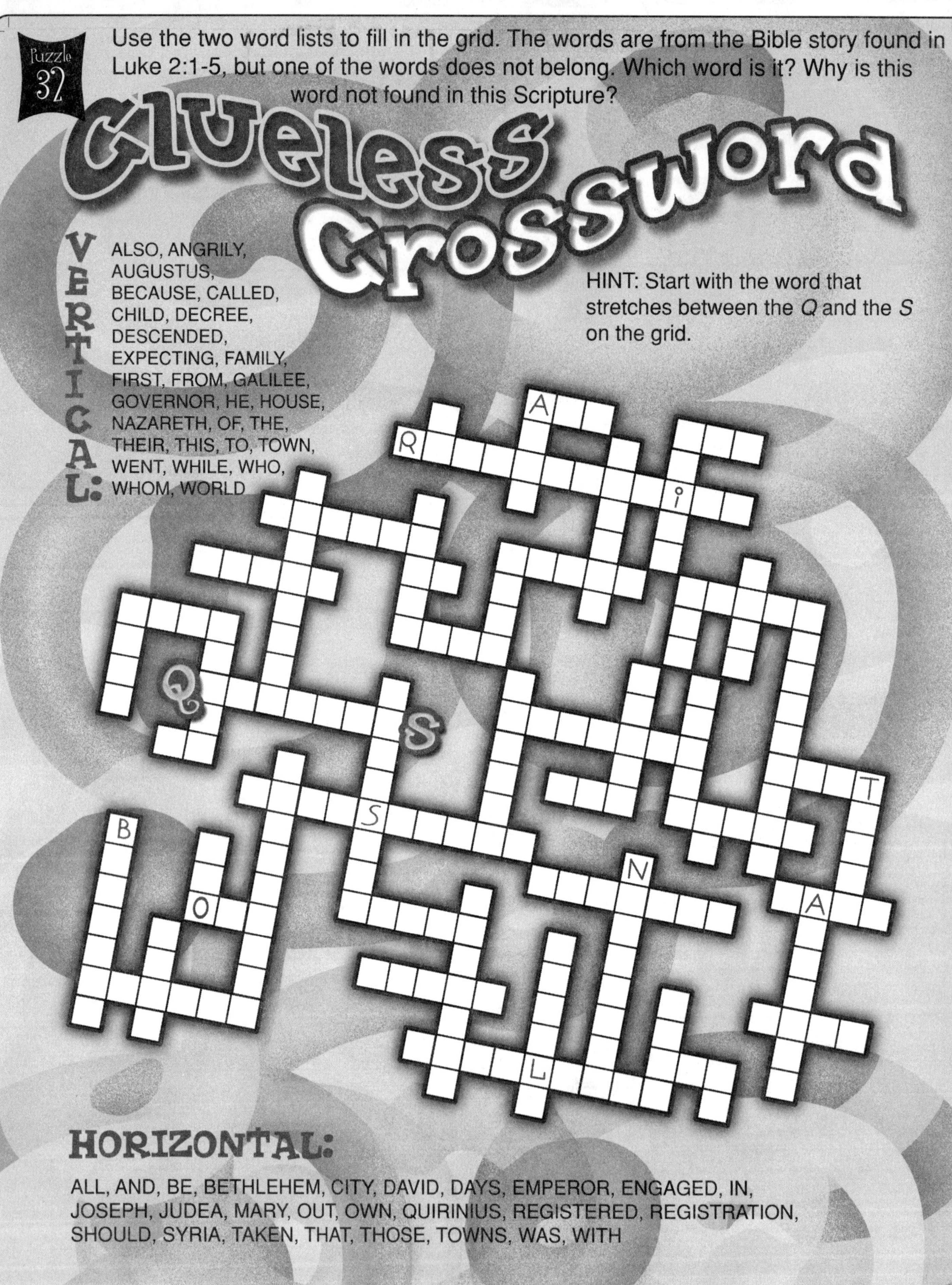

HORIZONTAL:

ALL, AND, BE, BETHLEHEM, CITY, DAVID, DAYS, EMPEROR, ENGAGED, IN, JOSEPH, JUDEA, MARY, OUT, OWN, QUIRINIUS, REGISTERED, REGISTRATION, SHOULD, SYRIA, TAKEN, THAT, THOSE, TOWNS, WAS, WITH

New Testament Puzzles (1), © 2008 Abingdon Press

 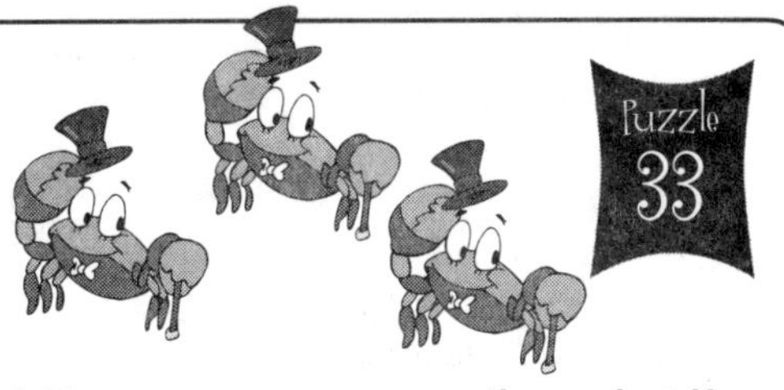

Trios

Find all the letters in the grid below that appear exactly alike three times. A letter may appear many times, but if it's in a different style, that doesn't count. You want only the trios (three exactly alike). Rearrange the combination of one letter from each trio to discover today's faith word.

_ _ _ _ _ _ _ _ _ _ _ _ _ _ _ _

A P N H W N Y Z D M

K B I S A A Y X P D

E Y P P N C Q B n A

Ψ A P O H A Ψ w L

H S P H X H H I f H

X W Y S I E G L P R

C C n S P N N R P O

X I H f B P X Q I T

w L D G D C Y E T Y

P K H L L M Z M U U

-THE VISIT-

Decipher the codes below to complete the story of an important visit.

After ___________ was born in ________________ of Judea, ________ __________

from the ________ came to ________________ asking, "Where is the ________ who has been

born king of the _________?"

___________ ___________ called these ________ __________ to come see him. He tried to get

them to tell him where the _________ was .

The __________ __________ continued their journey and stopped when the _________

they were following stopped. They entered the ___________ and found the _________ with

___________, his ____________. They __________ and paid him _________. They offered

him gifts of ________________, ___________________, and _____________. And having been

________ in a _________ not to return to ____________, they left for their own

_______________ by another ____________ .

A	B	C	D	E	F	G	H	I	J	K	L	M	N	O	P	Q	R	S	T	U	V	W	X	Y	Z

New Testament Puzzles (1), © 2008 Abingdon Press

Baptism

Baptism is a very special event. Solve the puzzle by searching the Scripture passages. When you read down the shells in order, you will discover what kind of an event baptism is.

1. Matthew 3:1—sixth word, sixth letter 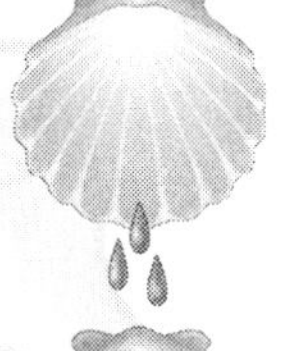

2. Matthew 3:13—tenth word, fifth letter 

3. Matthew 3:17—third word, fourth letter 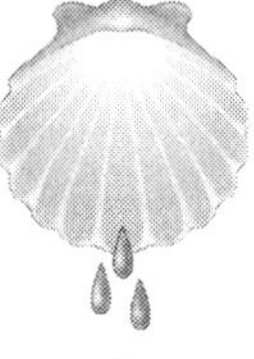

4. Mark 1:9—sixth word, second letter 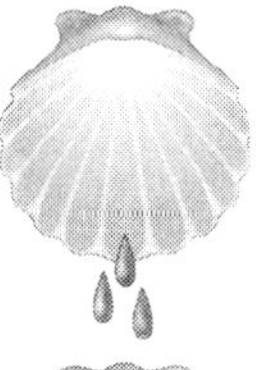

5. Mark 1:11—eighth word, first letter 

6. Luke 3:22—seventh word, third letter 

7. Luke 3:22—thirteenth word, fourth letter 

8. John 1:27—tenth word, first letter

9. John 1:28—fifth word, third letter 

CHOOSE A LETTER

1. the person here

2. to be

3. before a noun means "I own it"

4. boy child of a mother and father

5. in grammar it is an "article"

6. has a very special place in the heart

7. next to

8. which person

9. me

10. to be

11. very

12. happy

Find the words to Matthew 3:17b by choosing one letter from each of the letter groups to the right of the clue. For example, the answer to number 1 is **THIS**.

TLB AMH BUI GST

AOI NST

INM OYU

TBS ULO GBN

HTR NHO EYO

CBD EIO YLT OMW
VCG AIE DNT

MVW EIO YLT HNM

VWM THY AOE HNM

AOI

AOI MVW

MWV EIO GLD HNL

GPH HLM AEI IOA
SNT EIA GHD

THIS

____
____
____
____________ ,
____
____________ ,
____
____
____
____
____________ .

New Testament Puzzles (1), © 2008 Abingdon Press

JUMPiNG FiSH

Puzzle 37

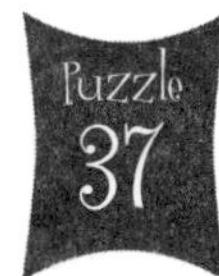

Follow the jumping fish. If you follow them in the correct order, you will discover what Mark 1:17 says. Be careful, though! Some stray fish got in the water!

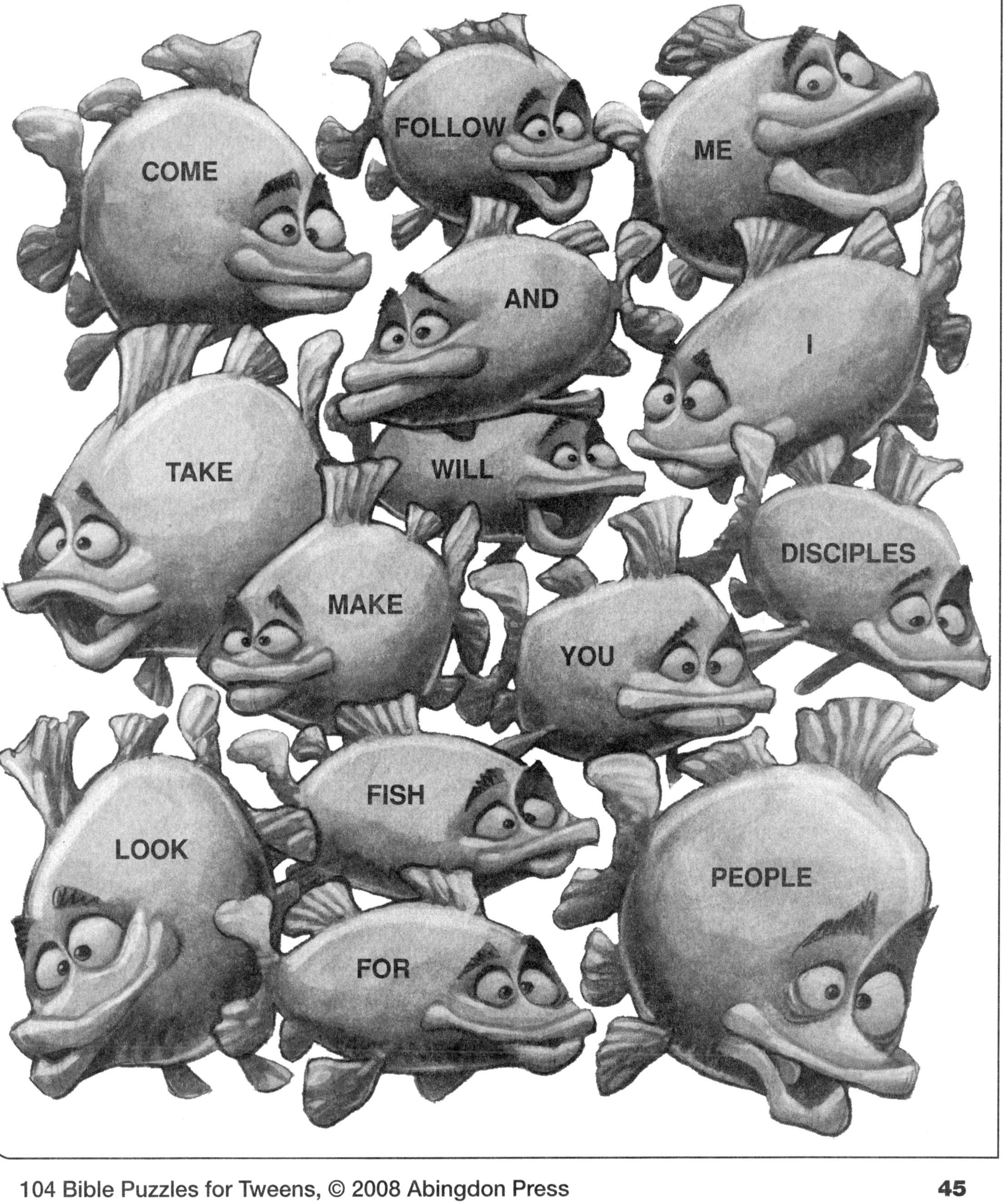

Disciples Acrostic

These New Testament people were Christian disciples. Can you take the hints and make their names spell **disciples**?

1. __ __ D __ __ __
2. __ I __ __ __ __ __
3. __ __ __ __ S
4. __ __ __ C __ __
5. __ __ I __ __ __
6. P __ __ __
7. L __ __ __
8. __ __ __ E __
9. __ __ __ __ __ __ __ S

CLUES:
1. One of the first disciples called. (Matthew 4:18)
2. Raised by his mother and grandmother in the faith. He traveled with Paul. (Acts 16:1)
3. His brother is John. They were often seen with Peter and Jesus. (Matthew 4:21)
4. Known for her good works. Peter raised her from the dead. (Acts 9:36-40)
5. One of the disciples, he baptized an Ethiopian court official. (Acts 8:26-38)
6. He was converted on the road to Damascus. (Acts 9:1-19) (Careful! We use his Roman name!)
7. He wrote the third Gospel.
8. The disciple who Jesus called the "rock." (Matthew 16:18)
9. Known for being short, this tax collector repaid everyone he had cheated fourfold. (Luke 19:2-10)

New Testament Puzzles (1), © 2008 Abingdon Press

SIGNS AND WONDERS

Read John 2:1-11 and then complete the puzzle.

1. mother of Jesus
2. followers of Jesus
3. one who serves another
4. another name for H_2O
5. the town where Jesus turned water into wine
6. the region where water was turned into wine
7. Turning water into wine ________ the glory of Jesus.

Did you discover another word hidden in the puzzle?

This Bible story is about Jesus' first

________.

(Write the hidden word in the spaces above.)

Weddings —Then and Now

Were weddings in Bible times anything like today's weddings? Take the true/false test below (just circle your answers) to test your knowledge of biblical weddings. Then look up the Bible passages to see how you did.

 T F

Music was forbidden at weddings. (Psalm 45:8)

The bride wore white. (Psalm 45:13-14)  T F

 T F

The bride wore a veil. (Genesis 24:65)

The bride had bridesmaids. (Psalm 45:14)  T F

 T F

The groom had a best man. (John 3:29)

People often came to weddings in their everyday work clothes. (Matthew 22:11-12)  T F

SERMON on the Mount

Some of these statements come from the Sermon on the Mount (Matthew 5–7); some come from other places in the Bible, and some come from places other than the Bible. Put an **S** before any statement that comes from the Sermon on the Mount. Put a **B** if it comes from somewhere else in the Bible, and put an **O** if it comes from somewhere other than the Bible.

_____ A wise child makes a glad father, but a foolish child is a mother's grief.

_____ Beware of false prophets, who come to you in sheep's clothing but inwardly are ravenous wolves.

_____ Blessed are the poor in spirit, for theirs is the kingdom of heaven.

_____ Do not boast about tomorrow, for you do not know what a day may bring.

_____ I destroy my enemy when I make him my friend.

_____ If you forgive others their trespasses, your heavenly Father will also forgive you.

_____ In everything do to others as you would have them do to you.

_____ It is better to deserve honors and not have them than to have them and not deserve them.

_____ Let your light shine before others, so that they may see your good works and give glory to your Father in heaven.

_____ Love is patient; love is kind; love is not envious or boastful or arrogant or rude.

_____ Love your enemies and pray for those who persecute you.

_____ No one can serve two masters.

_____ Owe no one anything.

_____ Whatever is begun in anger ends in shame.

_____ When anger rises, think of the consequences.

_____ For where your treasure is, there your heart will be also.

_____ You cannot shake hands with a clenched fist.

Hidden Words

Discover one of the Beatitudes by finding the hidden words in the picture below and putting them in the correct order. Read Matthew 5:9 to see if you are correct.

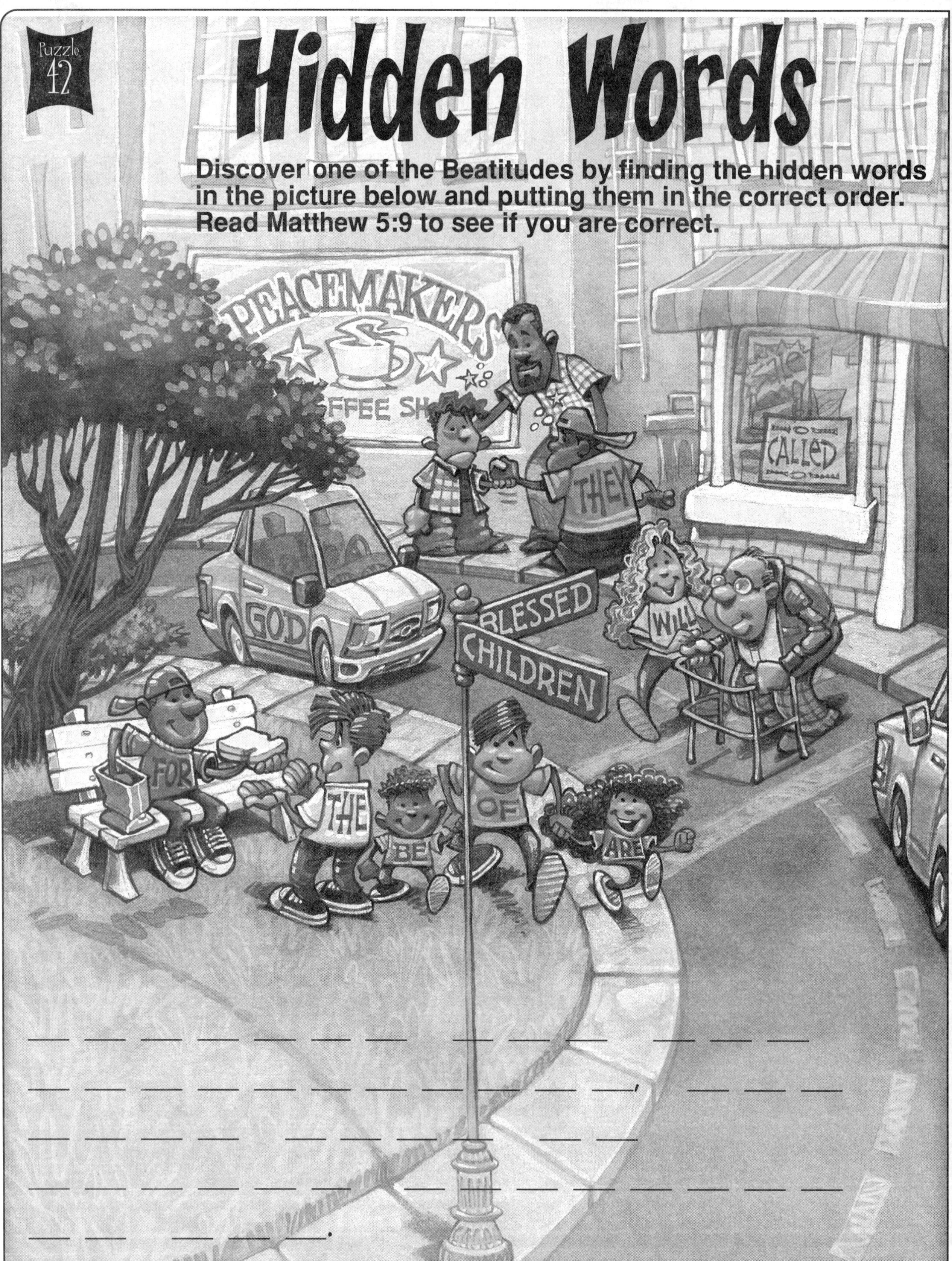

New Testament Puzzles (1), © 2008 Abingdon Press

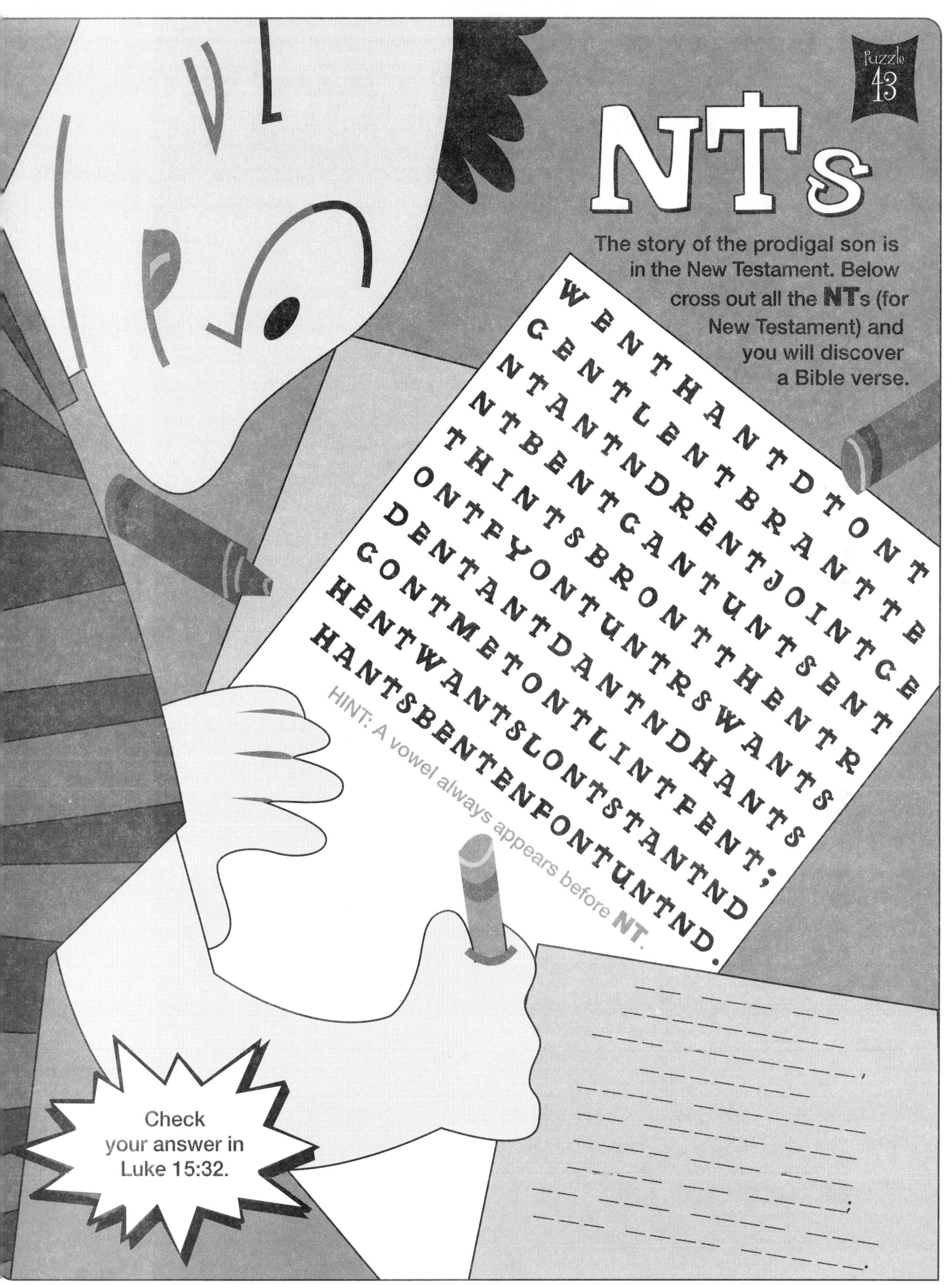

Puzzle 43

NTs

The story of the prodigal son is in the New Testament. Below cross out all the NTs (for New Testament) and you will discover a Bible verse.

WENTHANTDTONT
CENTLENTBRANTTE
NTANTNDRENTJOINTCE
NTBENTCANTUNTSENT
THINTSBRONTTHENTR
ONTFYONTUNTRSWANTS
DENTANTDANTNDHANTS
CONTMETONTLINTFENT;
HENTWANTSLONTSTANTND
HANTSBENTENFONTUNTND.

HINT: A vowel always appears before NT.

Check your answer in Luke 15:32.

Faithword

To discover an important word of faith, fill in the blanks in the words 1 through 10 with the correct missing letters. Transfer each letter to the matching numbered square.

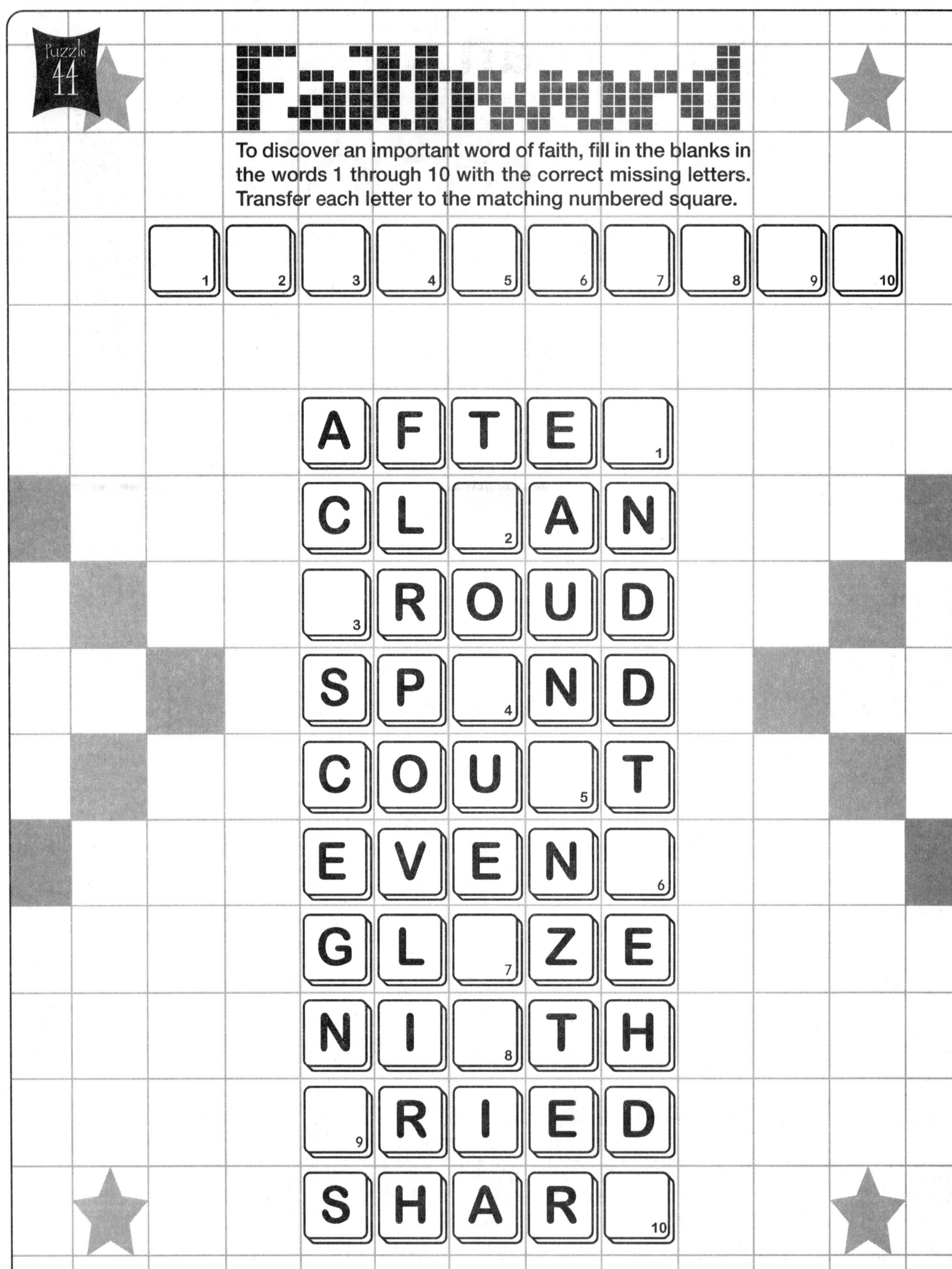

New Testament Puzzles (1), © 2008 Abingdon Press

More Than Enough?

Can you find two fish, five loaves of bread, and twelve baskets in this picture?
How about the number five thousand (5000)?

Follow the Lines

Follow the lines from the beginning letters of the Bible verse to the letters below. (Some letters will not be used.) Arrange the letters you discover in the correct order to complete the verse. Check John 6:35 to see if you are right.

I am the bread of life. Whoever comes to me will never be ____ ____ ____ ____ ____ ____, and

whoever believes in me will never be ____ ____ ____ ____ ____ ____ ____. (John 6:35)

New Testament Puzzles (1), © 2008 Abingdon Press

IT'S A MAZE!

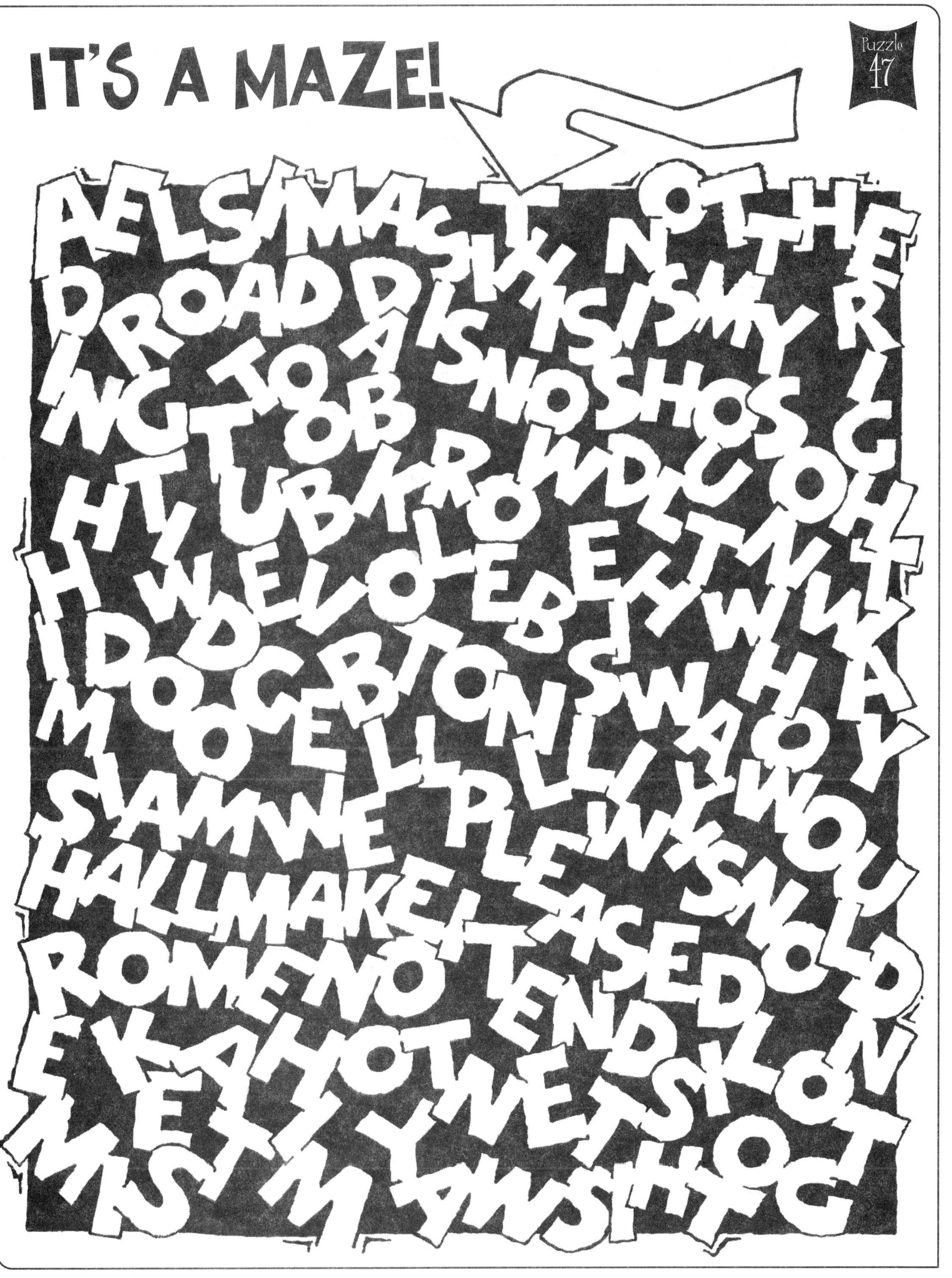

WHO IS JESUS?

Some of the names (titles) for Jesus have been separated.
Can you draw lines to bring them together again?

Need help? Look up the listed Scripture references.

New Testament Puzzles (1), © 2008 Abingdon Press

Sixteen Is the Number

9 x 3 =	8 + 8=	67 - 30 =	4 X 4 =	49 - 24 =	56 - 40 =	50 ÷ 5 =
S	I	P	A	F	M	N
32 ÷ 2 =	42 - 22 =	79 - 63 =	20 + 14 =	15 + 1 =	8 X 2 =	3 x 5 =
T	C	H	O	E	R	A
7 x 4 =	3+3+10 =	20 - 4 =	48 + 2 =	16 x 1 =	64 ÷ 4 =	64 - 48 =
G	E	S	D	U	R	R
18 - 2 =	49 ÷ 7 =	4 + 12 =	9 + 10 =	2 + 14 =	50 - 24 =	28 - 12 =
E	L	C	I	T	E	I
100 + 18 =	5 + 11 =	2 x 6 =	48 ÷ 3 =	25 - 9 =	63 - 39 =	51 - 27 =
H	O	Y	N	A	N	P
10 + 6 =	6 x 6 =	26 - 10 =	15 + 15 =	116 - 100 =	4 + 8 + 4 =	17 x 2 =
N	W	D	T	T	H	L
17 - 1 =	54 - 38 =	83 - 59 =	5 + 11 =	9 + 12 =	102 - 86 =	7 + 9 =
E	L	U	I	V	F	E

__ __ ____ ___ ____ ___

__ ___ ___ ____ __ ___.

It's a Miracle!

Or Is It?

Some of the stories in the New Testament are about miracles Jesus performed. Other stories are parables Jesus told. Do you know the difference? Read the very short descriptions of the stories below.

Put an **M** in front of each story that is about a miracle. Put a **P** in front of each story that is a parable. If you need some help, use the Scripture references listed below. Sometimes the Bible headings tell you which it is.

 At a wedding in Cana, water is changed into wine.

 Ten lepers are cured.

 A tiny mustard seed grows into a very large tree.

 Lazarus is raised from the dead.

 A shepherd leaves 99 sheep to look for the one that is lost.

 Blind men are given sight.

 Five thousand people are fed from 5 loaves of bread and 2 fish.

 People are invited to a wedding banquet, but they give excuses for not coming. A servant is then sent into the streets to gather guests.

 A Samaritan stops along the roadside to help a Jew who had been beaten and robbed.

Matthew 13:31-32; Matthew 14:13-21; Matthew 18:10-14; Matthew 20:29-34; Matthew 22:1-14; Luke 10:30-37; Luke 17:11-19; John 2:1-11; John 11:1-45

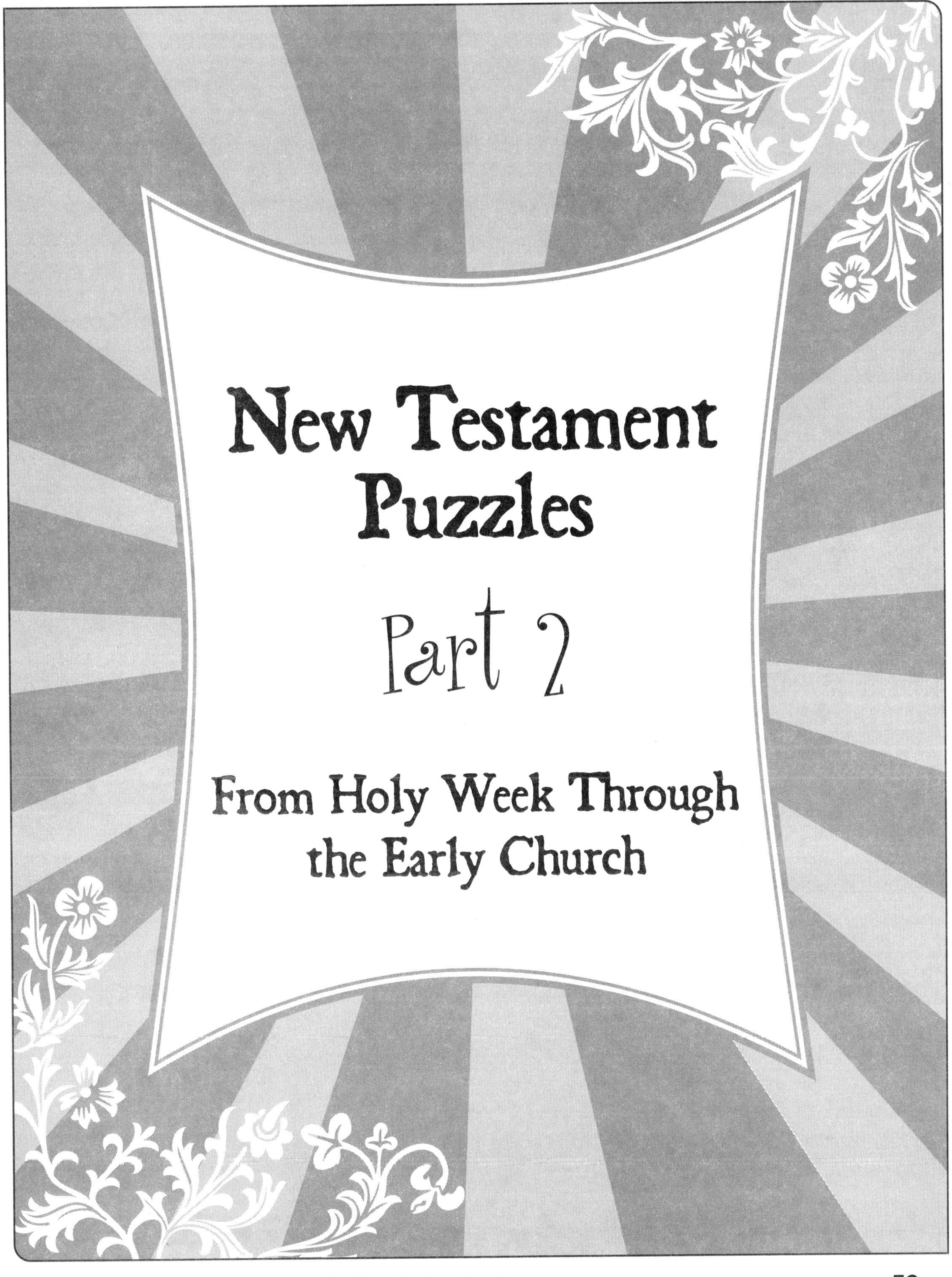

New Testament
Puzzles
Part 2
From Holy Week Through
the Early Church

PICTORIAL CROSSWORD

Discover some Palm Sunday words by using the first letter from each item pictured in the crossword to fill out the Bible puzzle below. Use the words you discover to fill out the clues.

DOWN:

1. ___ ___ ___ ___ ___

2. ___ ___ ___ ___ ___ ___

3. ___ ___ ___ ___ ___ ___ ___

ACROSS:

4. ___ ___ ___ ___

5. ___ ___ ___ ___ ___

6. ___ ___ ___

7. ___ ___ ___ ___ ___ ___

Letters and Numbers Math

Use the alphabet number code to the right and do the math to figure out what Matthew 21:11 says.

A	=	1
B	=	2
C	=	3
D	=	4
E	=	5
F	=	6
G	=	7
H	=	8
I	=	9
J	=	10
K	=	11
L	=	12
M	=	13
N	=	14
O	=	15
P	=	16
Q	=	17
R	=	18
S	=	19
T	=	20
U	=	21
V	=	22
W	=	23
X	=	24
Y	=	25
Z	=	26

$\overline{\text{Z - 6}}$ $\overline{\text{4 + D}}$ $\overline{\text{H + 1}}$ $\overline{\text{M + 6}}$ $\overline{\text{S - 10}}$ $\overline{\text{H + 11}}$ $\overline{\text{Y - 5}}$ $\overline{\text{A + 7}}$ $\overline{\text{C + 2}}$

$\overline{\text{O + 1}}$ $\overline{\text{L + 6}}$ $\overline{\text{Q - 2}}$ $\overline{\text{X - 8}}$ $\overline{\text{J - 2}}$ $\overline{\text{N - 9}}$ $\overline{\text{N + 6}}$

$\overline{\text{E + 5}}$ $\overline{\text{F - 1}}$ $\overline{\text{R + 1}}$ $\overline{\text{S + 2}}$ $\overline{\text{Z - 7}}$ $\overline{\text{G - 1}}$ $\overline{\text{I + 9}}$ $\overline{\text{J + 5}}$ $\overline{\text{W - 10}}$

$\overline{\text{J + 4}}$ $\overline{\text{C - 2}}$ $\overline{\text{U + 5}}$ $\overline{\text{Z - 25}}$ $\overline{\text{Q + 1}}$ $\overline{\text{F - 1}}$ $\overline{\text{Q + 3}}$ $\overline{\text{L - 4}}$ $\overline{\text{G + 2}}$ $\overline{\text{D + 10}}$

$\overline{\text{H - 1}}$ $\overline{\text{P - 15}}$ $\overline{\text{M - 1}}$ $\overline{\text{R - 9}}$ $\overline{\text{H + 4}}$ $\overline{\text{A + 4}}$ $\overline{\text{P - 11}}$

BY THE FIVES

Cross out every fifth letter to find out what the Scripture has to say. Read Matthew 6:33 to check your answer. Watch out—counting goes from one line to the next.

BUTSXTRIVLE

FIRYSTFONRTHEGKINGTDOM

OBFGODUANDHVIS

RIPGHTEZOUSNHESSALND

ALJLTHECSETHQINGSAWILL

MBEGIYVENTDOYOUJASWEGLL

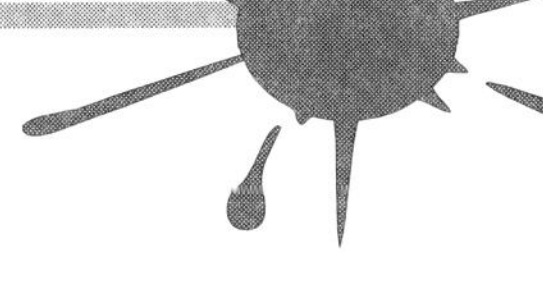

Invited by God

There are many places in the Gospels where God or Jesus personally invited individuals. There are also times when Jesus sent out others to carry the invitation. See if you can match the Scripture reference, who did the inviting, who they invited, and what they were invited to do. (Draw lines to match them up.)

OK! You caught us—*Jesus* and *disciples* are used more than once!

Luke 2:8-15
Matthew 2:1-11
Matthew 4:18-22
Luke 19:1-6
Luke 10:1-9
Mark 16:15-16

Jesus
angels
star led

shepherds
wise men
Simon Peter,
Andrew, James, and
John
Zacchaeus
disciples

find King
Come down; I must stay at
your house.
proclaim good news to
the world
cure sick; tell people about
the kingdom of God
find Savior
follow Jesus/fish for people

New Testament Puzzles (2), © 2008 Abingdon Press

COMMUNION SYMBOLS

Number the words in the correct order to discover what Matthew 26:28 says. Write the correct number in the circle beside each word. We've given you the first word.

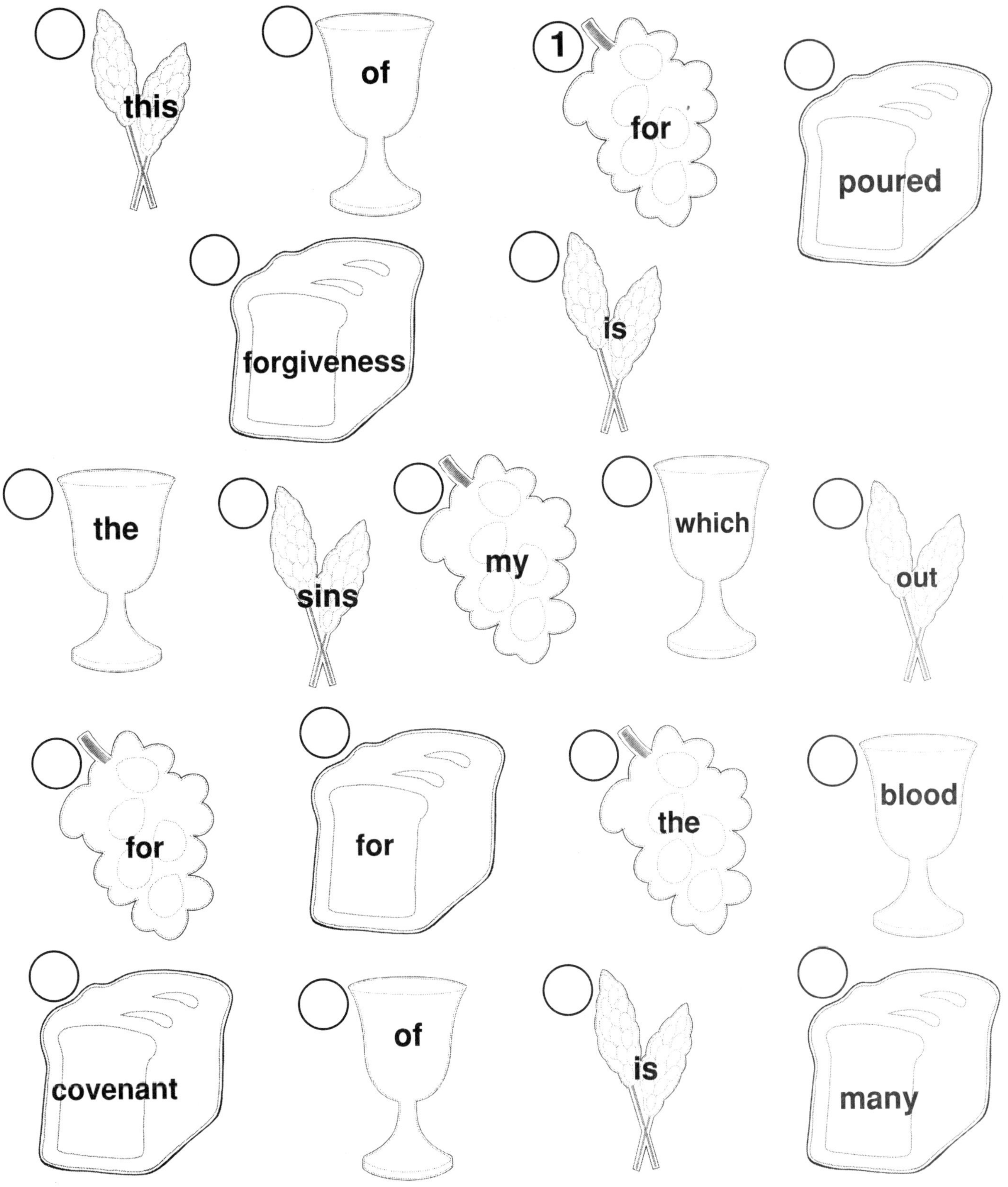

this

of

1 for

poured

forgiveness

is

the

sins

my

which

out

for

for

the

blood

covenant

of

is

many

Which Sacrament is it?

Trace the lines from the word *SACRAMENT* to the correct letters in the line below.
Then rearrange to discover the name of one of the sacraments of the church.

SACRAMENT

TMCMEUONINAO

_ _ _ _ _ _ _ _ _ _ _ _ _

Find your way to the garden: Read Mark 14:36b.

Jesus traveled from town to town healing people and sharing God's Word.
Follow today's verse to find Jesus in the garden.

Holy Week Word Search


```
L O R D T Q Y S B L E S S E D
C O I U R Z A E E B L H C G C
S U U R V N D L T U A R G S D
K O P C N T N P R R I C X O E
N X N A T H U I A I R E N N J
X O S O T R S C Y A T K A O E
D O I A F R M S A L E M O D R
H E E X Z D L I L Y E K F X U
S D N R I A A D M S E E V A S
I S N I I F P V H D A E R B A
Y N O D A C I T I B E W G S L
R G R R A L E C F D E Y L E E
P B Y K C G U W U X X L P W M
L A S T S U P P E R X O B U N
M O O R R E P P U F C H N N L
```

BETRAYAL
BLESSED
BREAD
BURIAL
CROSS
CRUCIFIXION
CUP

DEATH
DENIAL
DISCIPLES
DONKEY
GETHSEMANE
HOLY WEEK
HOSANNA
JERUSALEM

LAST SUPPER
LILY
LORD
PALM SUNDAY
SON OF DAVID
UPPER ROOM
TRIAL

New Testament Puzzles (2), © 2008 Abingdon Press

MISSING CONSONANTS

To discover what Psalm 86:5 says, place the missing consonants in the right order below. For this puzzle, *Y* will be considered a consonant. We've given you a head start.
(HINT: Read down, not across.)

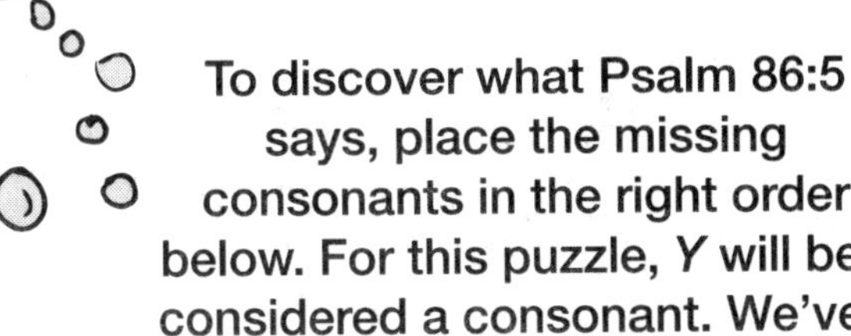

```
B  C    D D D D D     F F F    G G G G      H       L L L L L L
N N N N N      R R R R     S S    T T T    V V     W     Y Y
```

__ O __   A __ __   __ O

__ O U   F O __ __ I __ I __ G   A __ __

O   A B O U __ __ I __ __   __ __ O

__ O __ __   I __   __ A

A __ E   S __ E A __ __ A __ __   O __

__ O O __   __ O __ E   __ O U.

DENIAL TANGRAM

A tangram is a Chinese puzzle that uses shapes to make a picture.

Peter denied Jesus three times before the cock crowed twice (Mark 14:72). The rooster has become the symbol of Peter's denial.

Cut the shapes apart and see how quickly you can rearrange them to fill in the rooster.

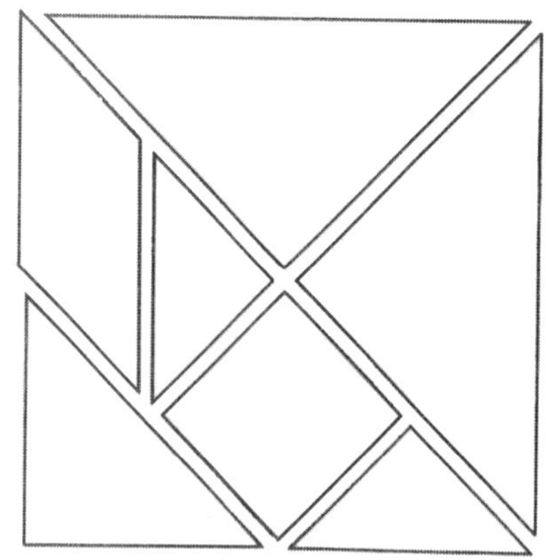

New Testament Puzzles (2), © 2008 Abingdon Press

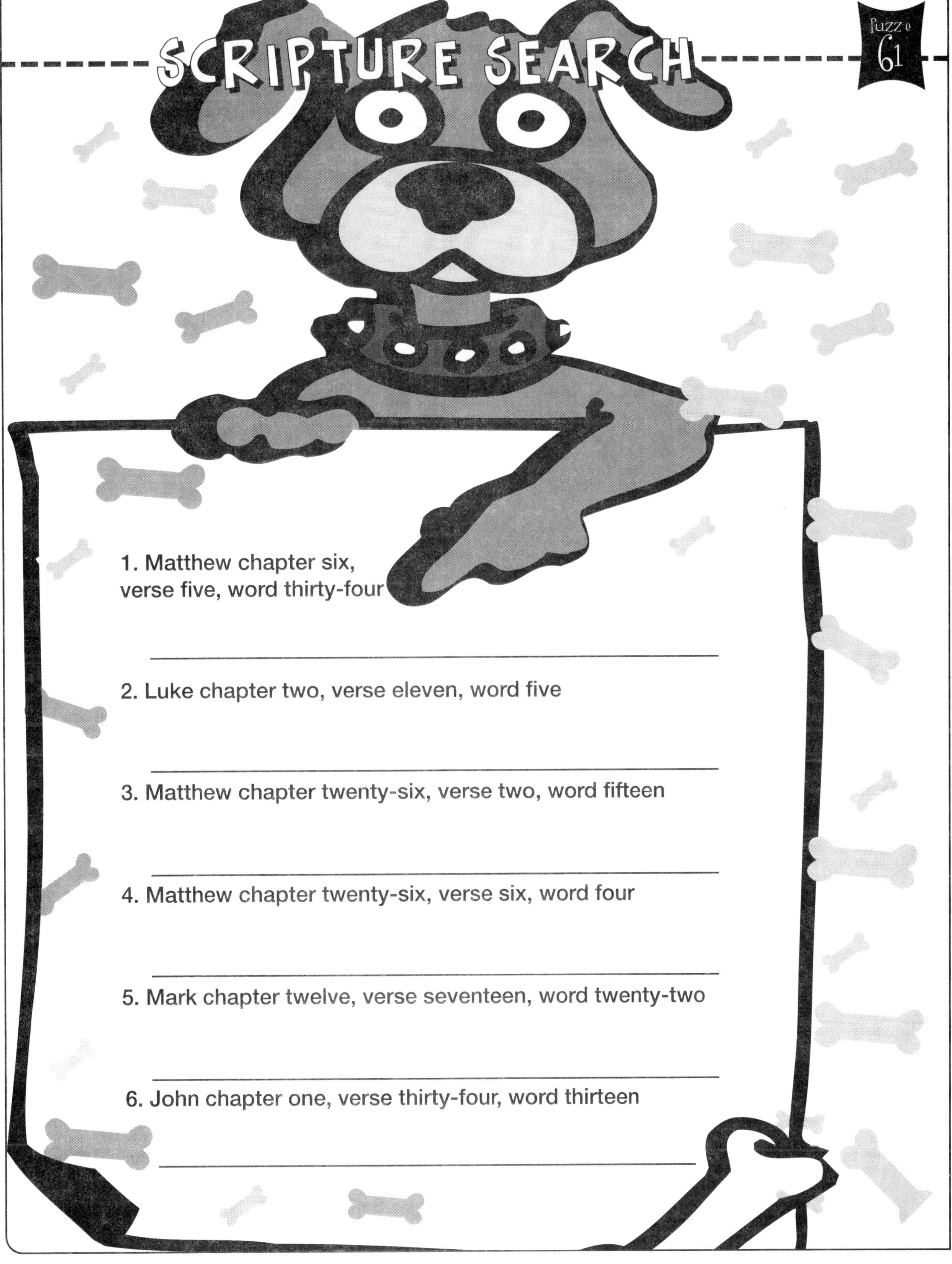

SCRIPTURE SEARCH

Puzzle
61

1. Matthew chapter six,
verse five, word thirty-four

____

2. Luke chapter two, verse eleven, word five

____

3. Matthew chapter twenty-six, verse two, word fifteen

____

4. Matthew chapter twenty-six, verse six, word four

____

5. Mark chapter twelve, verse seventeen, word twenty-two

____

6. John chapter one, verse thirty-four, word thirteen

____

Some of the events below took place during Holy Week. A few didn't. Put a check mark by each event that belongs in Holy Week and an *X* in front of any event that took place at a different time.

(Oh, by the way—to make it harder the events are not in order!)

You can skim through chapters 21–27 of Matthew if you need some help.

	Jesus cleanses the Temple.
	The shepherds visit Jesus in Bethlehem.
	Jesus is crucified.
	Jesus is tempted in the wilderness.
	Jesus and the disciples have the Last Supper in the Upper Room.
	Jesus teaches the disciples The Lord's Prayer.
	Peter denies Jesus three times.
	Jesus is arrested.
	The transfiguration of Jesus takes place before Peter, James, and John.
	Jesus prays in the Garden of Gethsemane.

GRAPH IT

Use the graph on page 74 to discover a great message.

Use a red or black pen or pencil to draw the message. The letter and number together give you a point on the graph. The letters are for the horizontal lines. The numbers are for the vertical lines. Find point H1. This is the spot where line H meets line 1. Place a small *x* at this point. Then find A1. Place a small *x* at this point. Draw a straight line to connect the two points. (You may need a ruler.) Then find A5. Repeat until you have connected all points in the first box. This gives you the first letter of the message. Repeat with each box.

H, 1	H, 6	H, 11	H, 16	H, 21	H, 27 1/2
A, 1	A, 6	A, 11	G, 16	F, 21	B, 27 1/2
A, 5	A, 7	A, 15	G, 17 1/2	F, 22	B, 26
C, 5	D, 7	E, 15	B, 17 1/2	G, 22	A, 26
C, 4	D, 9	E, 14	B, 16	G, 24	A, 30
B, 4	A, 9	H, 15	A, 16	E, 24	B, 30
B, 2	A, 10	H, 14	A, 20	E, 21	B, 28 1/2
G, 2	H, 10	E, 13	B, 20	A, 21	H, 28 1/2
G, 4	H, 9	E, 12	B, 18 1/2	A, 25	H, 27 1/2
F, 4	E, 9	H, 12	G, 18 1/2	C, 25	
F, 5	E, 7	H, 11	G, 20	C, 24	
H, 5	H, 7		H, 20	B, 24	
H, 1	H, 6	D, 12	H, 16	B, 22	
		B, 12		D, 22	
		B, 14		D, 25	
		D, 14		H, 25	
		D, 12		H, 21	

J, 6	J, 13
J, 10	J, 17
K, 10	L, 17
K, 8 1/2	L, 16
P, 8 1/2	K, 16
P, 10	K, 14
Q, 10	M, 14
Q, 6	M, 17
P, 6	Q, 17
P, 7 1/2	Q, 13
K, 7 1/2	O, 13
K, 6	O, 14
J, 6	P, 14
	P, 16
	N, 16
	N, 13
	J, 13

S, 1	S, 6	Z, 11	Z, 16	Z, 21
S, 5	S, 10	X, 11	S, 16	S, 21
W, 5	T, 10	X, 12	S, 20	S, 22
W, 4	T, 8 1/2	Y, 12	T, 20	W, 24
Z, 5	Y, 8 1/2	Y, 14	T, 17	S, 24
Z, 4	Y, 10	W, 14	V, 17	S, 25
W, 3	Z, 10	W, 11	V, 19	Z, 25
W, 2	Z, 6	S, 11	W, 19	Z, 24
Z, 2	Y, 6	S, 15	W, 17	V, 22
Z, 1	Y, 7 1/2	U, 15	Y, 17	Z, 22
S, 1	T, 7 1/2	U, 14	Y, 20	Z, 21
	T, 6	T, 14	Z, 20	
T, 2	S, 6	T, 12	Z, 16	
T, 4		V, 12		
V, 4		V, 15		
V, 2		Z, 15		
T, 2		Z, 11		

X, 28
S, 28
S, 29
X, 29
X, 28
Z, 28
Y, 28
Y, 29
Z, 29
Z, 28

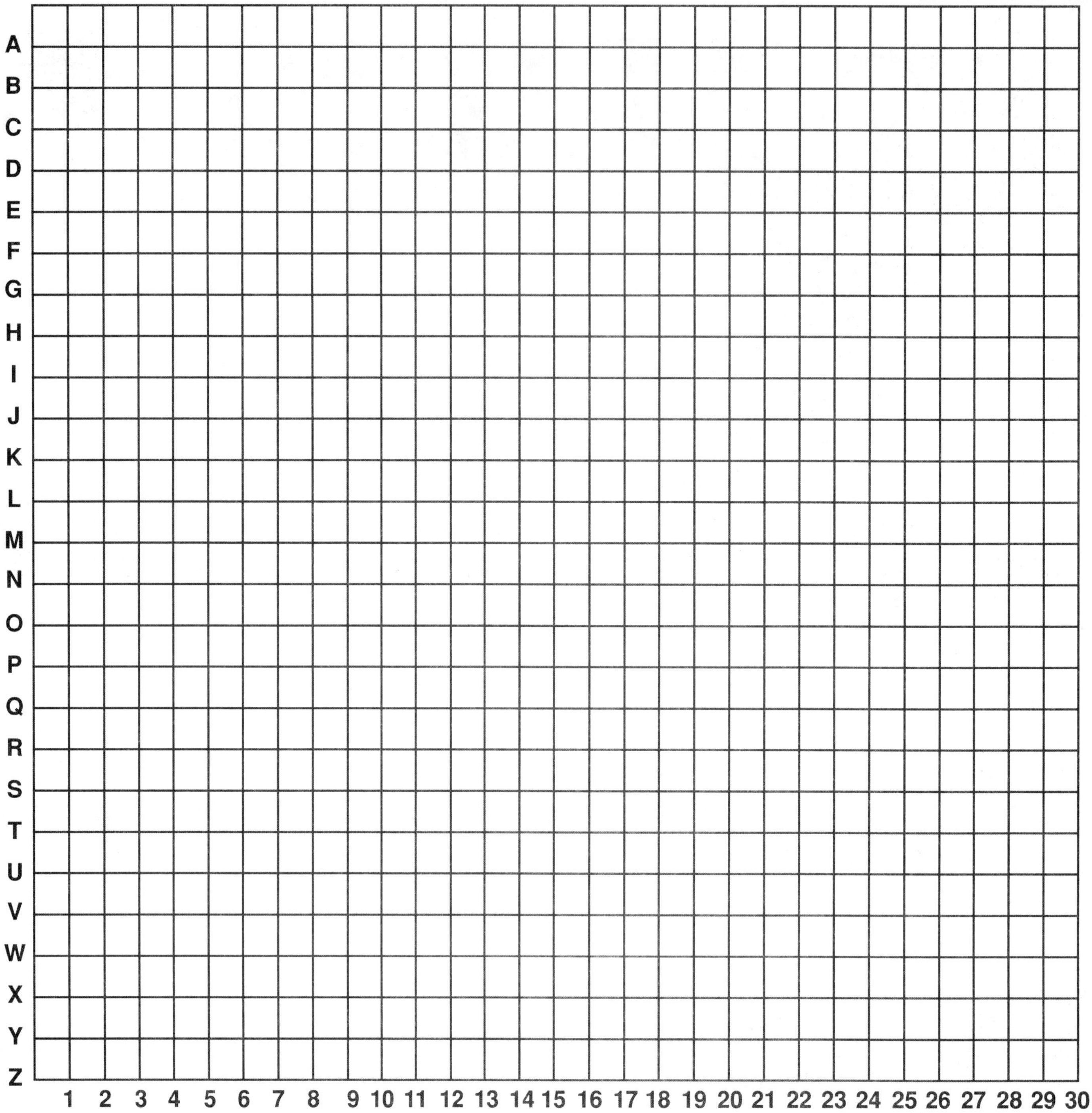

Puzzle 64

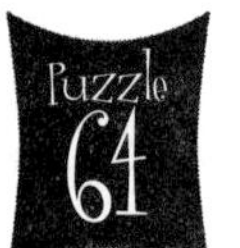

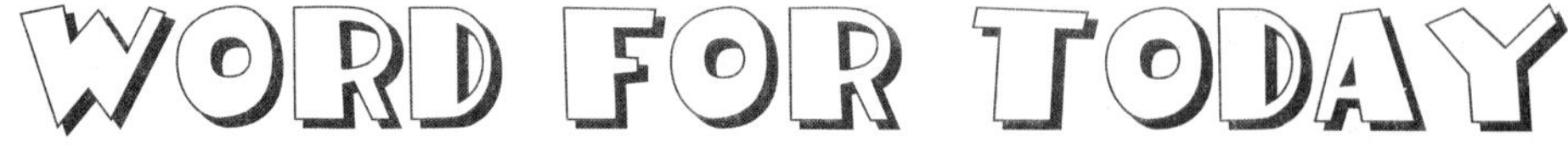

WORD FOR TODAY

Unscramble this word to discover what is so important about Easter Sunday.

I S R E T U R E O N R C

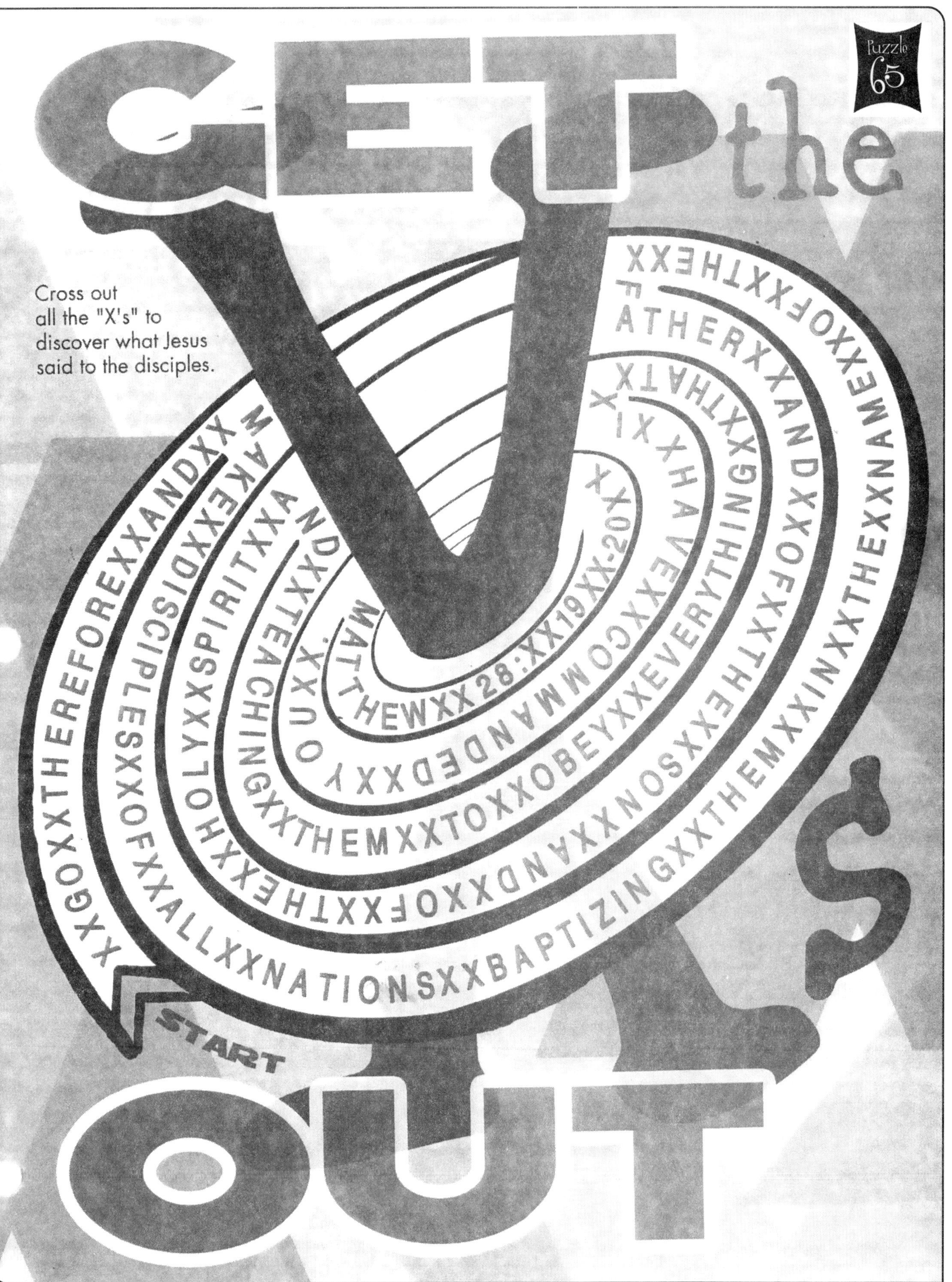
GET the
Puzzle 65
Cross out
all the "X's" to
discover what Jesus
said to the disciples.
START
OUT
XXGOXXTHEREFOREXXANDXXMAKEXXDISCIPLESXXOFXXALLXXNATIONSXXBAPTIZINGXXTHEMXXINXXTHEXXNAMEXXOFXXTHEXXFATHERXXANDXXOFXXTHEXXSONXXANDXXOFXXTHEXXHOLYXXSPIRITXXANDXXTEACHINGXXTHEMXXTOXXOBEYXXEVERYTHINGXXIXHAVEXXCOMMANDEDXXYOUXXTEACHINGXXTHEMXXTOXXOBEY
MATTHEWXX 28:XX19XX-20XX

10 Clues???

Read the 10 clues below to discover how Jesus was recognized by two men after the Resurrection.

Try to guess the answer in 5 clues. If you need more clues, turn the page upside down, and read clues 6-10.

 Clue # 1—Two men were walking on the road to a town about seven miles from Jerusalem.

 Clue # 2—Jesus walked with the two men on the road to Emmaus, but they did not recognize him.

 Clue # 3—They told Jesus about the Resurrection and Jesus explained that the Resurrection had been foretold in Scripture.

 Clue # 4—They asked Jesus to stay with them into the evening.

 Clue # 5—They then did something that people do every day.

 Clue # 10—Read Luke 24:35.

 Clue # 9—Jesus gave them the bread and their eyes were opened.

 Clue # 8—Jesus blessed the bread.

 Clue # 7—Jesus broke bread for the men.

 Clue # 6—Jesus sat at the table with the men.

Travels to Pentecost

At the Ascension of Jesus, the disciples were told that when the Holy Spirit came upon them they would be witnesses to the ends of the earth. Jews came from many nations to Jerusalem for the Pentecost festival. They were there when the Holy Spirit came to the disciples. Draw an arrow to Jerusalem from the homeland of each of the nations listed in Acts 2:9-11. These are just a few of the nations to which the disciples carried the good news.

Puzzle 67

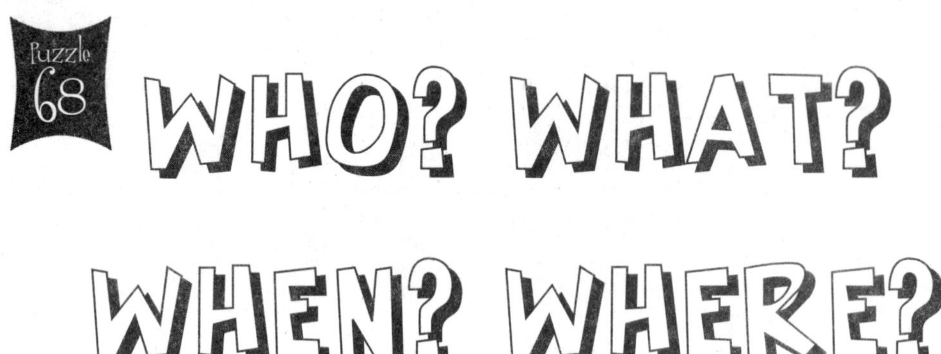

Fill in the blanks selecting words from the lists below. (A word can be used more than once.) Trying to be helpful, we have indicated below each blank the question you are answering. Watch out! We've given you extra words! Check your answers in Acts 1:8.

___________ will ___________ ___________ ___________ the ___________
Who?   What?   What?   When?   Who?

has ___________ upon ___________ ; and ___________ will be my ___________ in
    What?   Who?   Who?   What?

___________ , in all ___________ and ___________ , and to
Where?   Where?   Where?

___________ .
Where?

WHO?

Jesus
the disciples
Holy Spirit
him
you
them
we
Paul
Peter

WHAT?

go
come
witnesses
receive
give
power
strength
hope
decide

WHEN?

on the hour
6:00 pm
always
when
forever
tomorrow
last night
yesterday
never

WHERE?

Bethlehem
Judea
Tarsus
Jerusalem
Syria
Samaria
Nazareth
Rome
Egypt
the ends of the earth

New Testament Puzzles (2), © 2008 Abingdon Press

WHAT a MOUTHFUL!
Puzzle 69
On Pentecost the disciples spoke in many languages—the languages of the people who had come to the festival. Some of the words found in Acts 2:1-13 can be discovered in the words in the word bubbles. Hint: All the words are capitalized in the Scripture, and words are repeated only when they are also repeated in the Bible verses. Can you locate all 25 words?
ASI ACYR ENE
PEN TEC OST
JUD EAEG YPT
GALI LEA NS
ELA MIT ESG OD
MED ESLI BYA
PAM PHY LIA
HOL YSPI RIT
MESO POT AMIA
JE WSCR ETANS
PAR THI ANS
JER USA LEM
PHR YGIAJ EWS
SPIR ITAR ABS
PON TUSR OME
CAPP ADO CIA

SEARCH THE CHART

Circle the words in these locations:

1/A 1/E 1/H 1/J 2/A 2/E 2/J 3/B 3/F 4/E 4/J 5/B 5/F
5/G 6/A 6/C 6/J 7/C 7/E 7/G 8/A 8/B 8/F 9/E 9/F 9/H
10/A 10/C 10/E 10/F 10/G

	A	B	C	D	E	F	G	H	J
1	receive	say	knelt	live	and	so	is	Spirit	one
2	baptized	communion	up	both	sins	now	in	soon	be
3	for	of	when	now	they	forgiven	know	trust	come
4	down	my	under	God	the	above	John	did	of
5	Messiah	Jesus	live	prayed	in	repent	Christ	slow	mine
6	so	then	that	yours	by	to	care	and	your
7	others	help	every	give	may	to	be	tell	Lord
8	and	you	right	wrong	need	will	have	our	those
9	heart	love	remember	keep	name	the	trial	gift	treasure
10	of	forgiven	you	by	the	Holy	in	his	forever

Then rearrange the words below to discover the verse. Check your answer by reading
Acts 2:38. Hint: We've given the location of each word below also.

5/F	1/E	7/G	2/A	7/C	1/J	4/J

8/B	10/G	9/F	9/E	10/A	5/B	5/G

6/A	6/C	6/J	2/E	7/E	2/J	3/F

8/A	10/C	8/F	1/A	10/E	9/H	3/B

4/E	10/F	1/H

     New Testament Puzzles (2), © 2008 Abingdon Press

PEOPLE PUZZLES

Read Acts 2:43-47 to find the missing words. Then fill in the puzzles.

Awe came upon everyone, because many wonders and __6__ were being done by the apostles. All who believed were together and had all things in common; they would __1__ their possessions and __3__ and distribute the __7__ to all, as any had need. Day by day, as they __9__ much __8__ together in the temple, they __4__ __5__ at home and ate their food with glad and generous hearts, __2__ God and having the goodwill of all the people. And day by day the Lord added to their number those who were being __10__.

The early Christians devoted themselves to

_ _ _ _ _ _ _ , _ _ _ _ _ _ _ _ _ _ _ ,

and _ _ _ _ _ _ _ .

Read Acts 2:42 in your Bible to check your answer. Talk with your leader and fellow tweens about how your church does these same things today.

1. Cover the graph with a blank piece of paper.
2. Slide the paper to the right until you uncover the first letter marker (△, ☺, etc.).
3. Write the letter in the first blank of the answer.
4. Continue sliding the paper and writing the letters until you have all the letters to spell out the four things that the early Christians devoted themselves to.

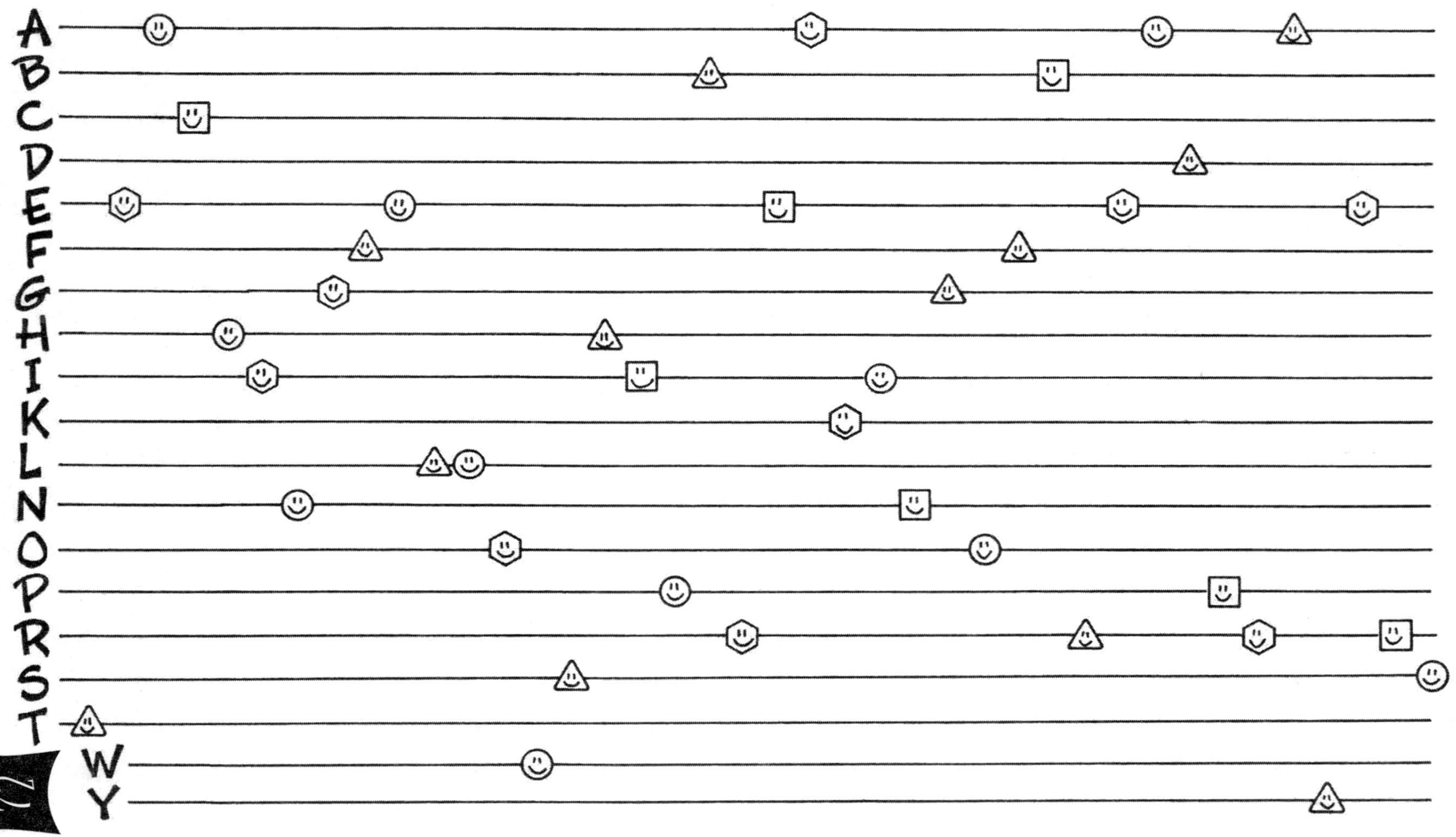

A
B
C
D
E
F
G
H
I
K
L
N
O
P
R
S
T
W
Y

Puzzle 72

Seven Chosen

The early church soon learned it needed to divide up the work if everything was going to get done. They chose seven people for a special task. You will find their names in Acts 6:5. Most are very unusual names. Look the names up in the Scripture and then figure out which nazme fits in each number below. We have given you one letter for each name.

THE LONG AND THE SHORT OF IT

The Scripture below has words of all sizes. Use the list to help you discover what the Scripture says. Having trouble? Read 1 Corinthians 12:4-7. We've decided to give you a head start by putting in a few letters here and there.

two letters	three letters		four letters	five letters	eight letters
in	all	God	each	gifts	services
is	and	now	good	given	everyone
is	and	the	Lord	there	
it	are	the	same	there	nine letters
of	are	the	same	there	activates
of	are	the	same		varieties
of	but	the	them	six letters	varieties
of	but	the		common	varieties
of	but	who		Spirit	
to	for			Spirit	ten letters
					activities

thirteen letters
manifestation

N ___ ___   ___ ___ ___ ___ ___   R ___   ___ ___ ___ ___ ___ ___ ___ ___ ___   ___ ___

___ ___ F ___ ___,   B ___ ___   ___ ___ ___   ___ ___ ___ ___   S ___ ___ ___ ___ ___ ___;

___ N ___   ___ ___ ___ ___ ___ ___   A R ___   ___ ___ ___ ___ ___ ___ ___ ___ ___   ___ ___ ___

___ ___ ___ ___ ___ ___ ___ ___ ___,   ___ ___ T   ___ ___ ___   ___ ___ ___ ___   L ___ ___ ___ ___;

___ N ___   ___ ___ ___ ___ ___ ___   R ___   ___ ___ ___ ___ ___ ___ ___ ___ ___   ___ ___ ___

___ ___ ___ ___ ___ ___ ___ ___ ___ ___,   ___ U ___   ___ T   S ___ ___   ___ ___ ___ ___

___ ___ ___ ___   G ___ ___   W ___ ___   A ___ ___ ___ ___ ___ ___ ___ ___ ___   ___ ___ L

___ ___   ___ H ___ ___   ___ N   E ___ ___ ___ ___ ___ ___ ___.   T ___   ___ ___ ___ ___ H

___ S ___   ___ V ___ ___ ___   ___ ___ ___   ___ ___ ___ ___ ___ ___ ___ ___ ___ ___ ___ ___

___ ___ ___   ___ ___ ___ ___   ___ P ___ ___ ___ ___   ___ O ___   ___ ___ ___ ___

___ ___ ___ ___ ___ ___ ___ ___ ___ ___ ___   G ___ ___ D.

A Different Message

Three words in each group are related. Select the one that is different in each group, then put them in order on the lines below. The words will give you a message from Paul. Check the message in 2 Timothy 4:7.

1. mine	I	yours	theirs
2. have	give	take	work
3. live	take	sleep	fought
4. three	four	two	the
5. good	sweet	sour	salty
6. forgive	fight	love	help
7. I	we	they	them
8. jump	skip	dance	have
9. started	begun	finished	initiated
10. book	door	chair	the
11. sit	stand	race	sleep
12. him	her	she	I
13. have	where	when	why
14. kind	nice	kept	polite
15. on	by	in	the
16. score	count	time	faith

__________ __________ __________ __________

__________ __________ , __________ __________

__________ __________ , __________

__________ __________ .

What's It Mean?

Match the Christian symbol with its meaning.

secret sign early Christians drew to show they were Christians

Symbol for Jesus—the beginning and the end (alpha and omega)

the sign of the wise men

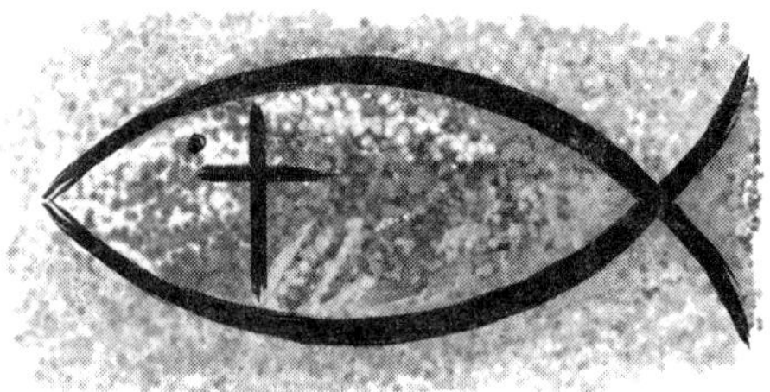

symbol for the Crucifixion

symbol of the resurrection/ symbol for Christian

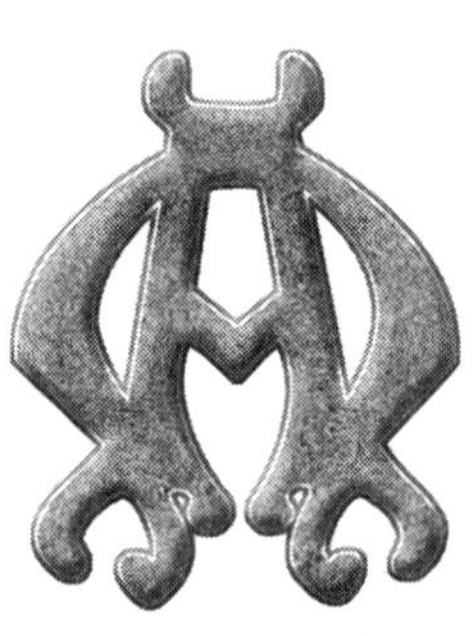

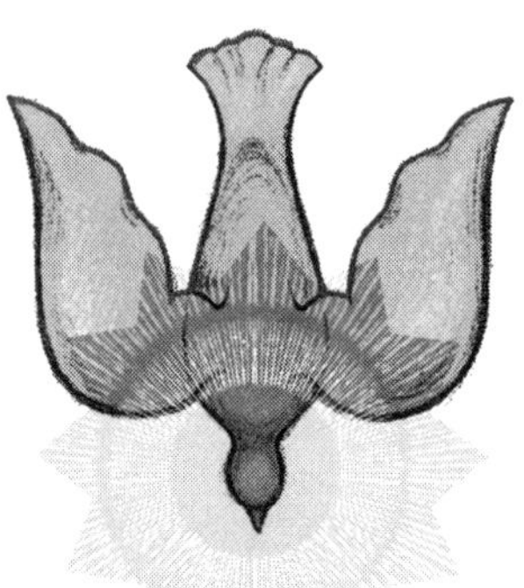

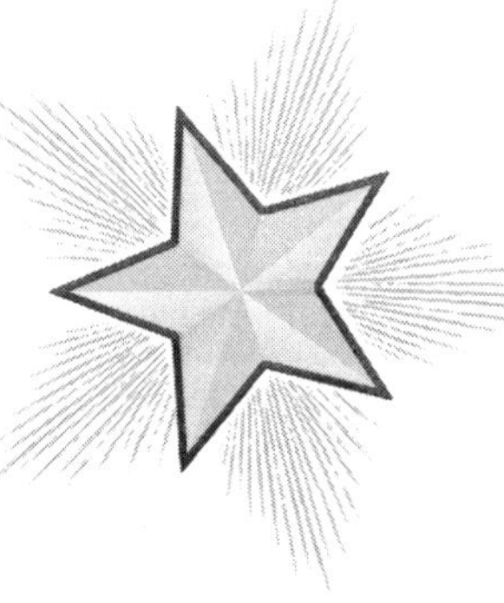

symbol for new (or young) Christians (those whose faith is just budding)

baptism

Holy Spirit

Where In The World?

Puzzle 77

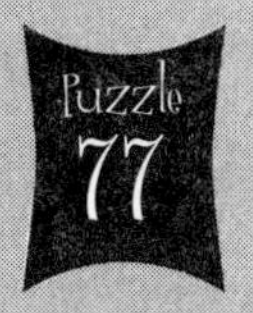

The disciples were given the task of spreading the Good News to everyone. Who were some of the people they took the message to? Write the name of the Christian convert on the map beside the place he or she was from. Use the Scripture references scattered around the map to discover the correct answers.

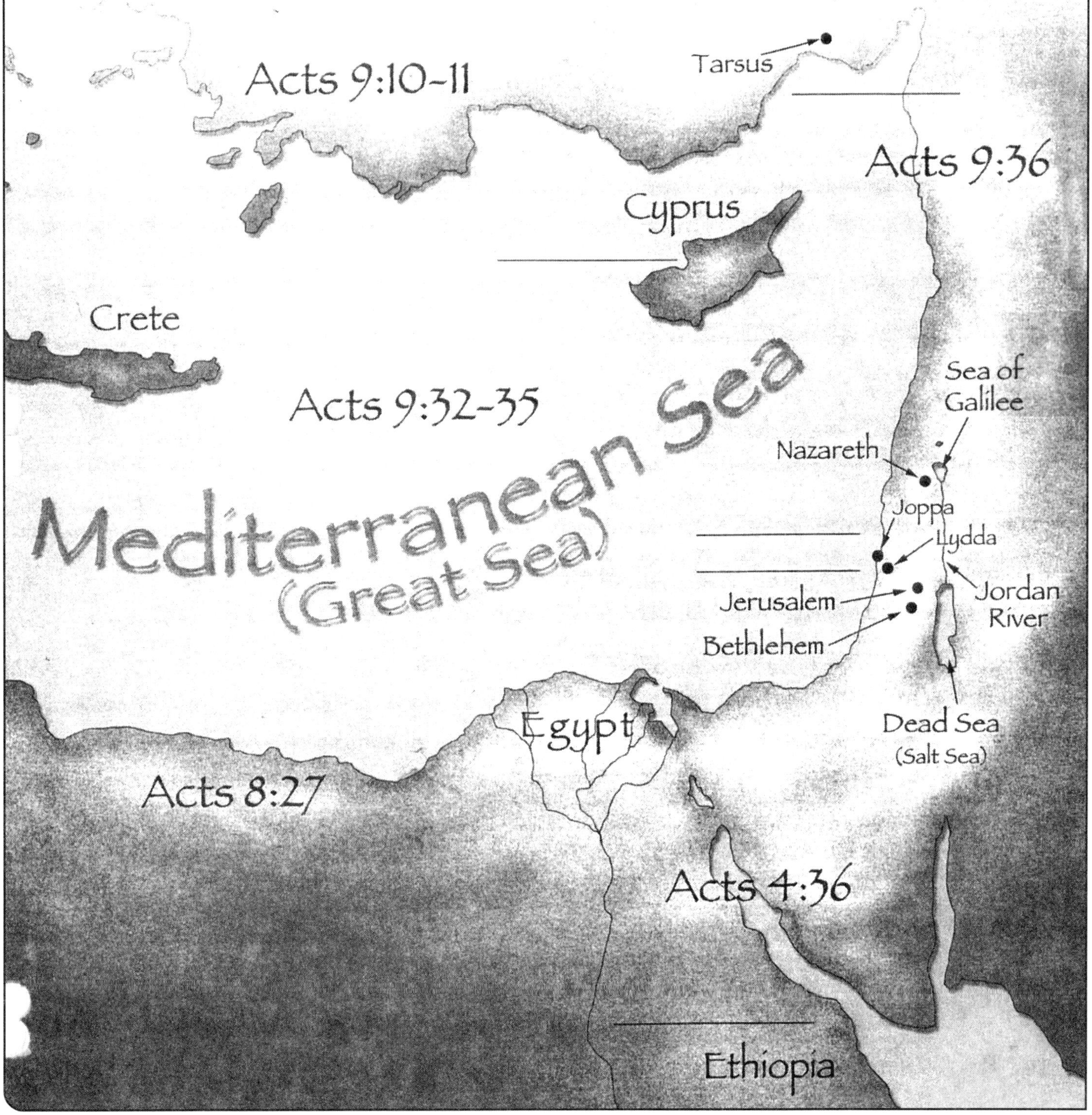

Categories

Fill in the chart below with names that fit the category and that begin with the letter at the top of the chart.

NOTE: Do not use the names of prophets in the Old Testament Person category—use them only in the Old Testament Prophet category.

	A	I	J	M	N
Old Testament Person					
Old Testament Prophet					
One of the Twelve Disciples					
Believers in Jesus					

BEWARE! **One of these answers has a trick to it.**

If you need a little help, use these hints:
1. Look at the list of the books of the Bible at the front of your Bible.
2. A last name can be used.
3. For a list of the disciples see Matthew 10:1-4. (Nathanael is thought by some people to be the last name of one of the disciples. See John 1:45.)
4. You'll find one name in Acts 9:10.
5. You've probably never heard of this person from Romans 16:15.
6. Read John 19:39.

     New Testament Puzzles (2), © 2008 Abingdon Press

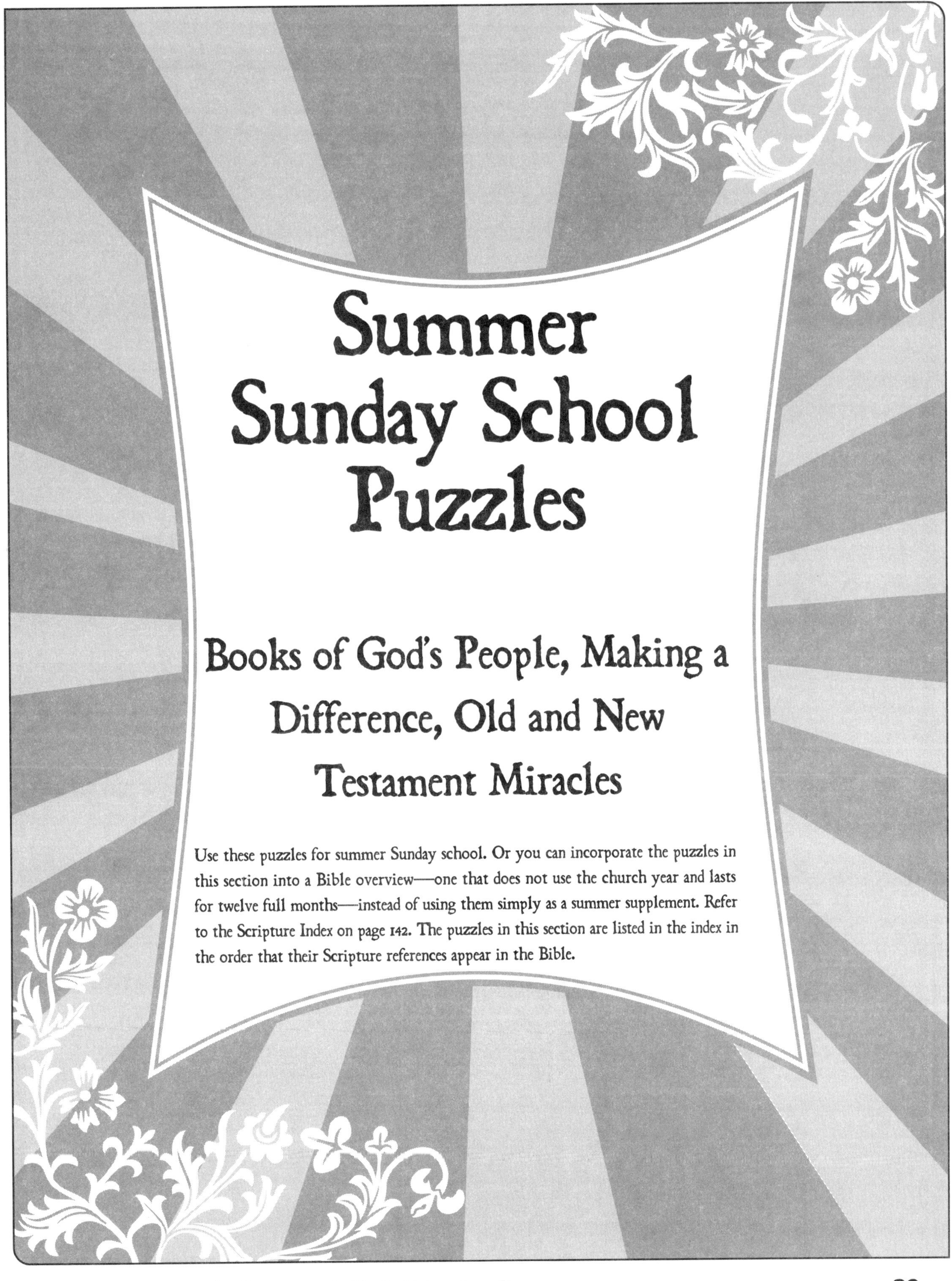

Summer Sunday School Puzzles

Books of God's People, Making a Difference, Old and New Testament Miracles

Use these puzzles for summer Sunday school. Or you can incorporate the puzzles in this section into a Bible overview—one that does not use the church year and lasts for twelve full months—instead of using them simply as a summer supplement. Refer to the Scripture Index on page 142. The puzzles in this section are listed in the index in the order that their Scripture references appear in the Bible.

Coded

107:1

YOUR NAME

In Bible times, people who were educated spoke both Greek and Hebrew. Here are both alphabets and the sound each letter makes. Can you write your name in Greek and Hebrew?

GREEK

Letter	Name	Sound
A	ALPHA	A
B	BETA	B
Γ	GAMMA	G
Δ	DELTA	D
E	EPSILON	E
Z	ZETA	Z
H	ETA	Ē
Θ	THETA	TH
I	IOTA	i
K	KAPPA	K, C
Λ	LAMBDA	L
M	MU	M
N	NU	N
Ξ	XI	X
O	OMICRON	O
Π	PI	P
P	RHO	R
Σ	SIGMA	S
T	TAU	T
Y	UPSILON	U, Y
Φ	PHI	PH
X	CHI	CH
Ψ	PSI	PS
Ω	OMEGA	Ō

HEBREW

Letter	Name	Sound
א	ALEPH	'
ב	BETH	B
ג	GIMEL	G
ד	DALETH	D
ה	HE	H
ו	WAW	W
ז	ZAYIN	Z
ח	HETH	H/KH
ט	TETH	T
י	YOD	Y
כ	KAPH	K
ל	LAMED	L
מ	MEM	M
נ	NUN	N
ס	SAMEKH	S
ע	AYIN	'
פ	PE	P
צ	TSADHE	TS
ק	QOPH	Q
ר	RESH	R
שׂ	SIN	S
שׁ	SHIN	SH
ת	TAW	T

Summer Sunday School Puzzles, © 2008 Abingdon Press

			D		E			D		N	S			
	A	I	E		K	I	N	D	U	O	I	F		
	I	L	G	H	F	E	O	U	S	L	S	S	E	
W	H	O	L	N	T	R	H	P	N	R	E	U	S	
W	R	N	A	V	D	I	N	O	N	E	R	S	E	S

						R	■	P						
■	R							U						■
■				■	K								■	■
				■					■					■
■	■	■				■	H					■	■	■

Puzzle 81

Book of WISDOM

Rearrange each set of letters to fit in the boxes below them and you will discover a piece of wisdom from Proverbs 21:21. (We've put in a few letters to get you started.)

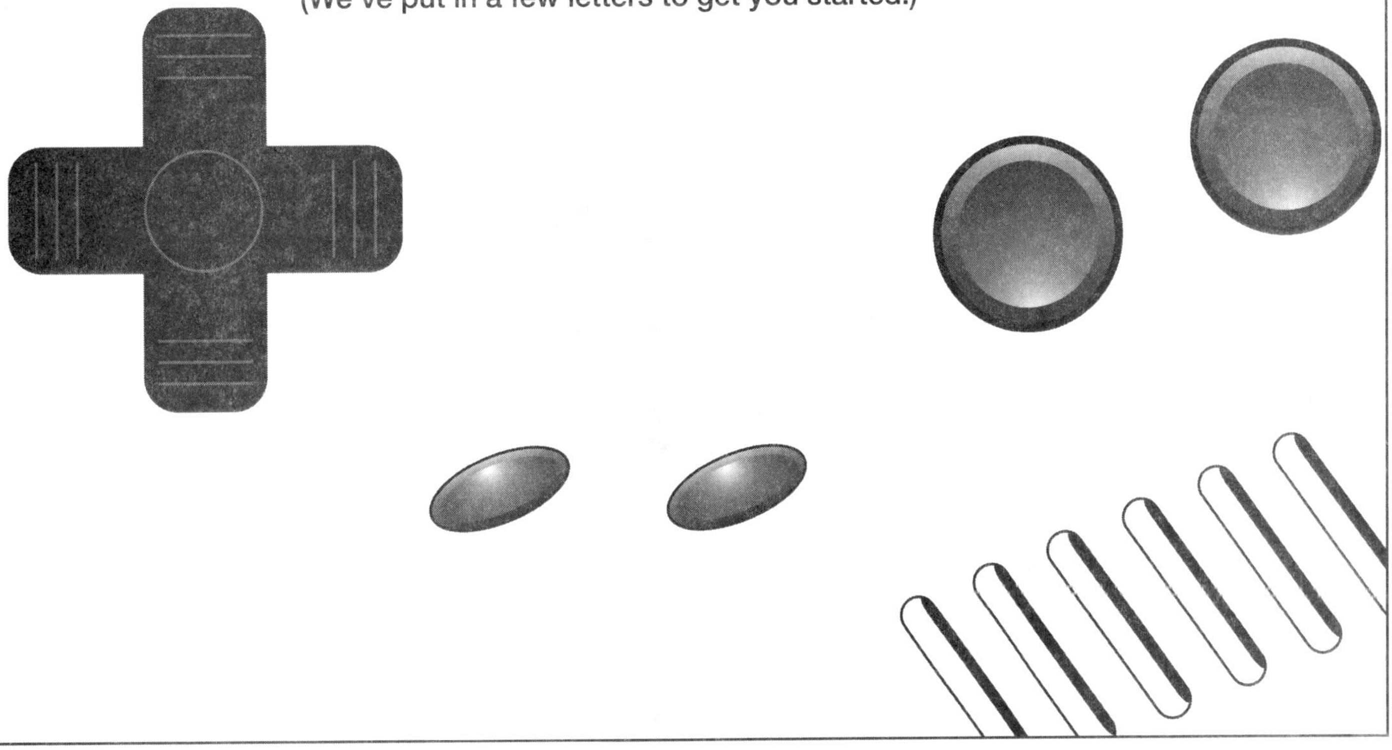

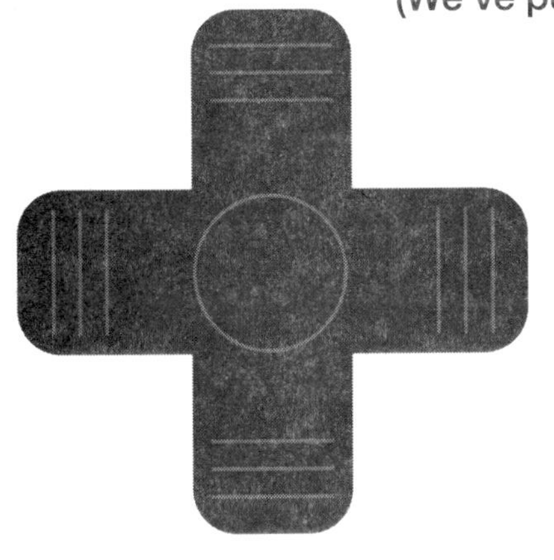

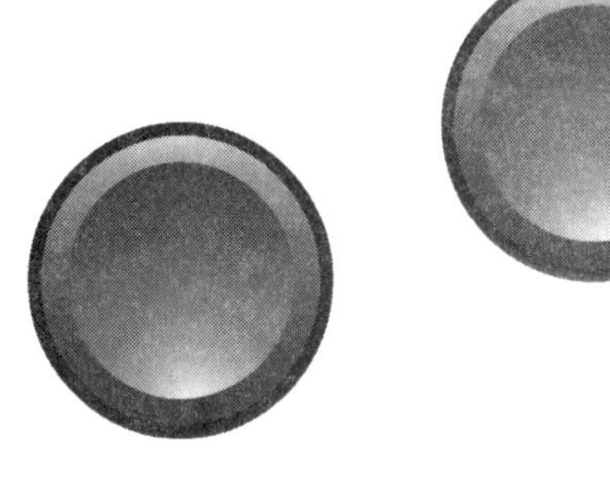

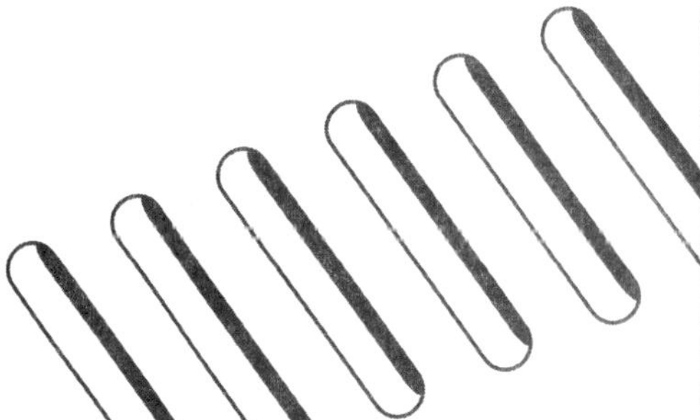

Proverbial Sudoku

Solve the Sudoku puzzle to discover in which chapters and verses in Proverbs the Proverbs below are found. The first number in a line across will be the chapter number; the second will be the verse number.

	3	6	9	5		7	4	2
2	5	7	1	3	4		9	
	8	9	6	7	2		3	5
3			8	6		5	2	9
9	2	8			5	6	7	4
	6	5	4	2	9	3		8
8	7			4	6	9	5	
5		2	7	8	3	4		1
6	4	3	5	9			2	8

Note: To solve a Sudoku, numbers 1 through 9 must appear in both rows across and down. There can be no repeat of numbers in either line.

1. Hear, my child, your father's instruction, and do not reject your mother's teaching. Proverbs ____ : ____

2. Hear, for I will speak noble things, and from my lips will come what is right. Proverbs ____ : ____

3. Listen, children, to a father's instruction, and be attentive, that you may gain insight. Proverbs ____ : ____

4. Leave the presence of a fool, for there you do not find words of knowledge. Proverbs ____ : ____

5. My child, do not forget my teaching, but let your heart keep my commandments. Proverbs ____ : ____

6. My child, keep my words and store up my commandments with you. Proverbs ____ : ____

7. No one finds security by wickedness, but the root of the righteous will never be moved. Proverbs ____ : ____

8. Lay aside immaturity, and live, and walk in the way of insight. Proverbs ____ : ____

9. The fear of the LORD is the beginning of knowledge; fools despise wisdom and instruction. Proverbs ____ : ____

Un-crossword Puzzle

The Letters of the New Testament give us truth we can live by. They give us good advice and hope. What encouragement is most common in these Letters? Find out by completing the answers in the puzzle below.

DOWN ONLY

1. Do not neglect to show ________ to strangers. (Hebrews 13:2)

2. Be quick to listen, slow to speak, slow to __________. (James 1:19)

3. May ________, peace, and love be yours in abundance. (Jude 2)

4. ________ your faith with goodness. (2 Peter 1:5)

5. We are surrounded by so great a cloud of _____. (Hebrews 12:1)

6. Let us ________ one another. (1 John 4:7)

7. The fruit of the Spirit is love, joy, peace, ______ . . . (Galatians 5:22)

8. ______ in hope. (Romans 12:12)

9. The peace of God . . . will guard your ________ . . . (Philippians 4:7)

New Testament Advice

The Letters of the New Testament give us lots of practical advice. Choose the numbered statement that matches each New Testament book below. Write that number in the proper square. When all your answers are correct, the total of the numbers will add up to be the same number across each row and down each column. What is that number? __________

1. This book tells us about the fruit of the Spirit. (chapter 5, verse 22)
2. This book tells us to put away falsehood and speak the truth to our neighbors. (chapter 4, verse 25)
3. This book says that Paul "fought the good fight, . . . finished the race, . . . [and] kept the faith." (chapter 4, verse 7)
4. This book tells us, "Rejoice in hope, be patient in suffering, persevere in prayer. Contribute to the needs of the saints; extend hospitality to strangers." (chapter 12, verses 12 & 13)
5. This book says, "Let us love, not in word or speech, but in truth and action." (chapter 3, verse 18)
6. Verse 14 in chapter 12 of this book tells us to "pursue peace with everyone."
7. Chapter 3 of this book tells us to have compassion, kindness, humility, meekness, and patience. (verse 12)
8. *Don't be selfish and conceited, but be humble* is the message of this book. (chapter 2, verse 3)
9. The whole of chapter 13 of this book is about how Christians are supposed to love.

Add Across →

Add Down ↓

Colossians ______	2 Timothy ______	1 John ______
Ephesians ______	Romans ______	1 Corinthians ______
Hebrews ______	Philippians ______	Galatians ______

Summer Sunday School Puzzles, © 2008 Abingdon Press

Follow the STAR

Throughout the Bible we find references to stars and their importance. Again in Revelation, a star is mentioned. Follow the path through the stars and learn Jesus' words of love.

START

I

am

ROOT

THE

of

AND

DESCENDENT

THE

DAVID

MORNING

STAR.

BRIGHT

THE

Check your answer in Revelation 22:16-17.

Answer:

ALL STRETCHED OUT

Today's Bible verse is all stretched out. Turn your paper sideways, stand back a few paces, and read what Revelation 1:8 says.

Summer Sunday School Puzzles, © 2008 Abingdon Press

Puzzle 87

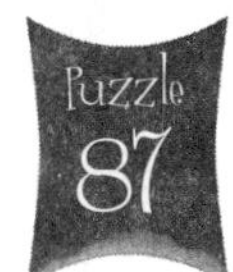

Scrambled Family Tree

Unscramble the names on the family tree below.
If you have trouble, check Ruth 1:1-4 and 4:21-22.

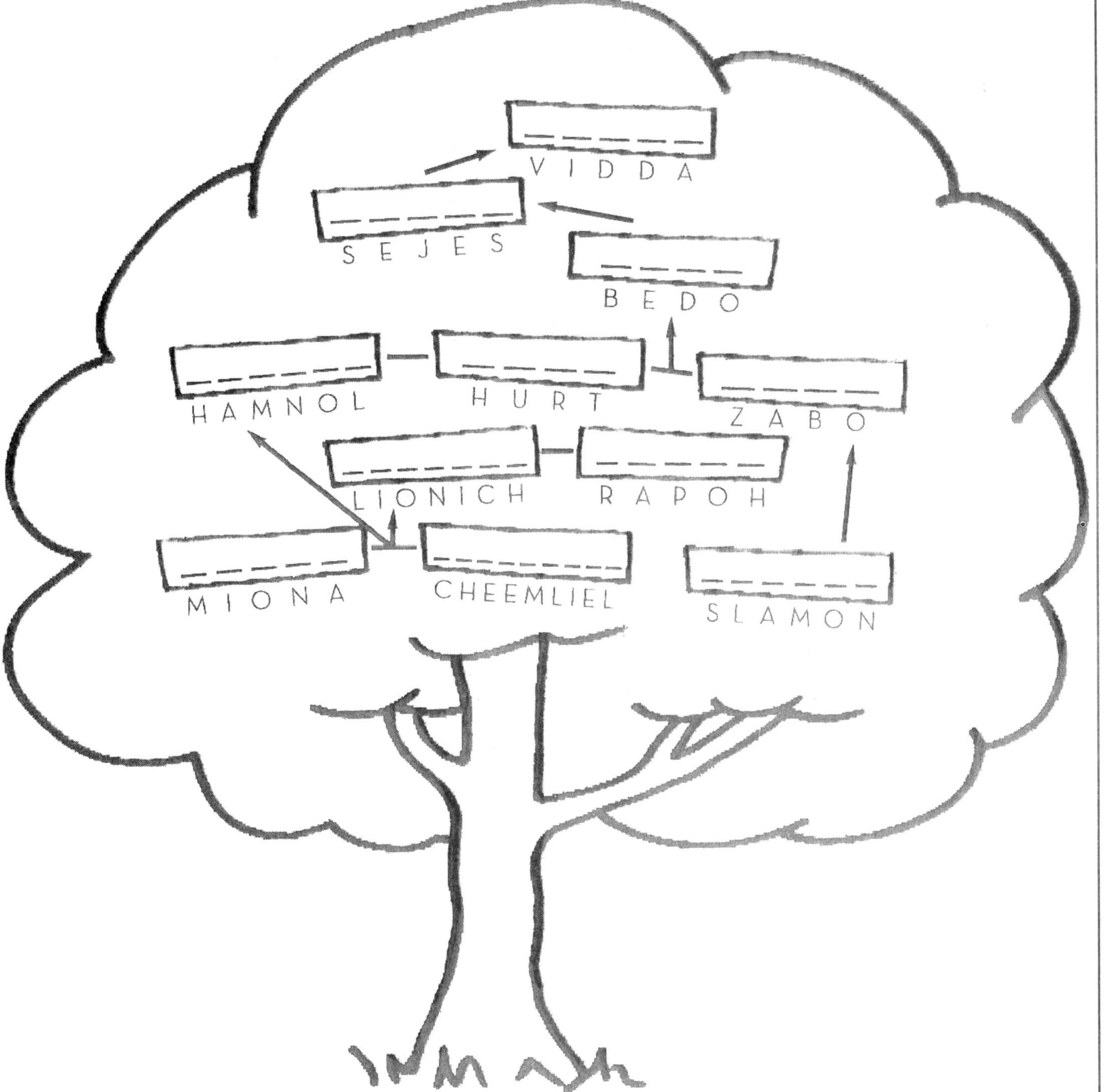

Encouragement

1 Thessalonians 5:11 has 14 words. The number of letters in each word is shown under each answer blank below. The letters for each word are in a straight line reading up, down, forward, backward, or diagonally. The last letter of one word is somewhere next to the first letter of the next word. The answer is one continuous line through each of the words. Lines never cross, and a letter may be used only one time. Begin at the arrow pointing down. That will give you a nine-letter word. Then when you get to the end of that word, look for another nine-letter word with a letter that begins next to the last letter of the first word.

```
↓ A A G A A E R A U A B A A A A S
H B B P L E D B B O B O B B B T B
E C U C C O C C C Y C C C Y C C C
R D D D I E D D D D E E D N I S D
E P G N E F E E G E E Y E E E A R
F F G F F G F U F F F F T F N F E
O G W G G H G G U G Z G O G Z G H
R H H G R I H H H Y X W H M H H T
E E I I I J I I I I I P E A C H O
J J N J J K J J J Q J U J J J J J
K K K C K L K K K K K D L I U B D
L L L L O U L L L L D L L L C L N
A M C M M U M W M T Y Z S M M M A
N N N N N O R N N E A N O T H E R
O O L O O P O A O N O N O Z O Y O
P P P P P Q P P G O P P P P P P P
W V Q L Q R Q P Q E Q Q V Q Q W Q
U R R P R W R R R R Z R R Y R R S
```

________ ________ ___ ______ ___
  9   9   3   7   3

_____ __ ____ _____ ' __
  5   2   4   5   2

______ ___ ___ _____.
  6   3   3   5

Summer Sunday School Puzzles, © 2008 Abingdon Press

Samuel's Answer

Find all the letters that go with each shape. Unscramble the letters to spell a word. When you have all the words, you will know Samuel's answer to God found in 1 Samuel 3:10.

Y

S

L

S

E

V

O

O

S

N

I

A

S

E

F

R

U

P

R

G

E

R

N

I

T

K

T

N

I

A

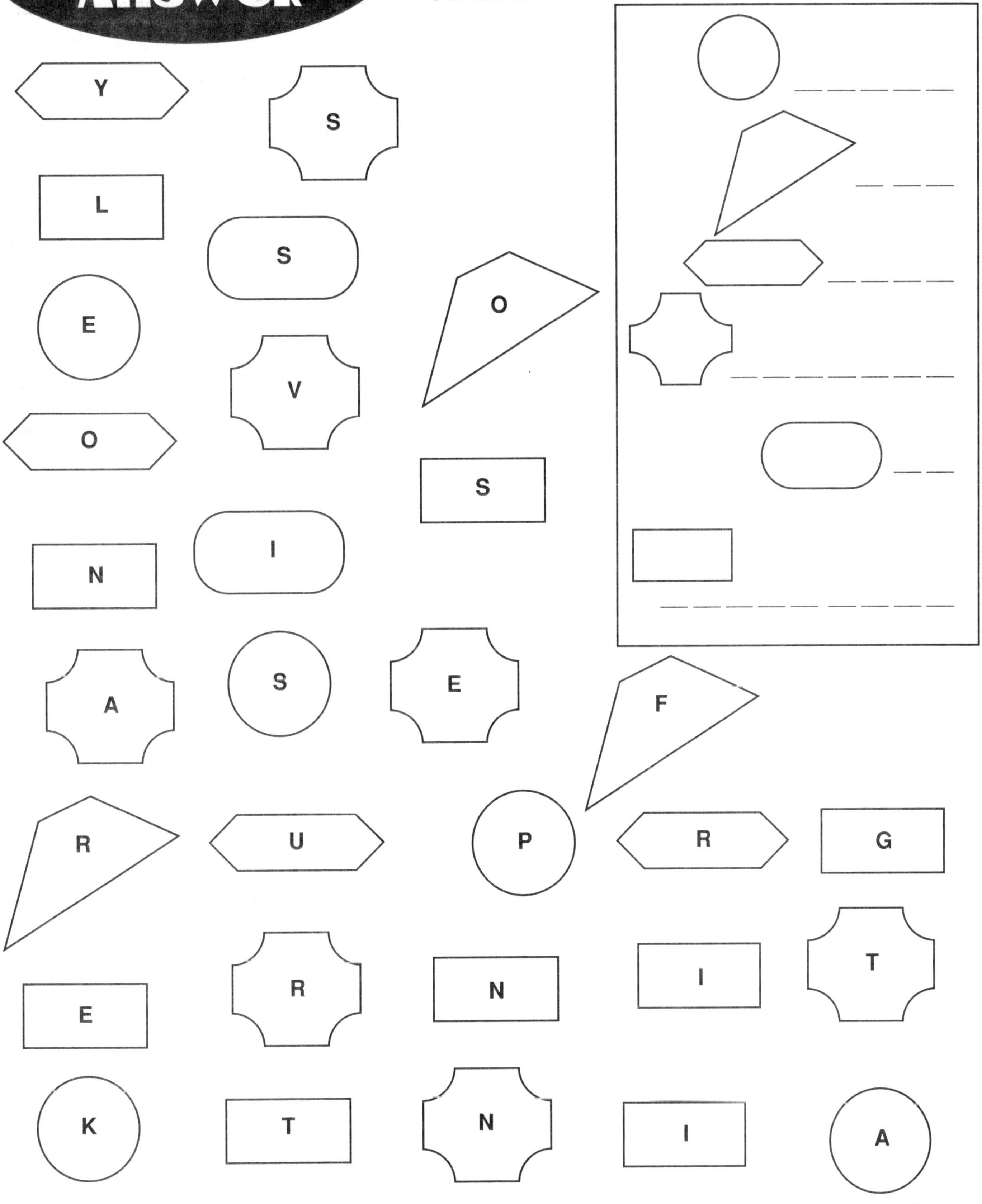

Which Testament?

How many can you get right?

Below are the names of some people who have made a difference. Do you know whose story is told in the Old Testament and whose is told in the New Testament? Put OT or NT before each person.

1. Abigail—She made peace between David and her husband Nabal.

2. Lois and Eunice—They raised Timothy in the faith.

3. Elijah—He was a prophet for God.

4. Abraham—He was the ancestor of a multitude of nations.

5. Deborah—She was a judge.

6. Zacchaeus—He repented of his sins and paid back those he had cheated four-fold.

7. The boy who shared his lunch.

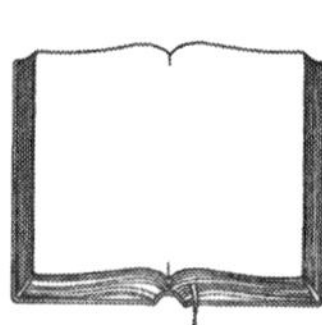

8. Ruth—She stayed with her mother-in-law, worshiped God, and became the mother of Obed.

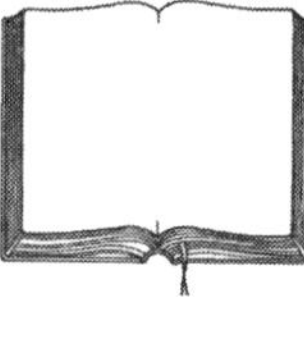

9. Hannah—She was the mother of Samuel and dedicated her son to God.

10. Stephen—He was chosen to serve the church.

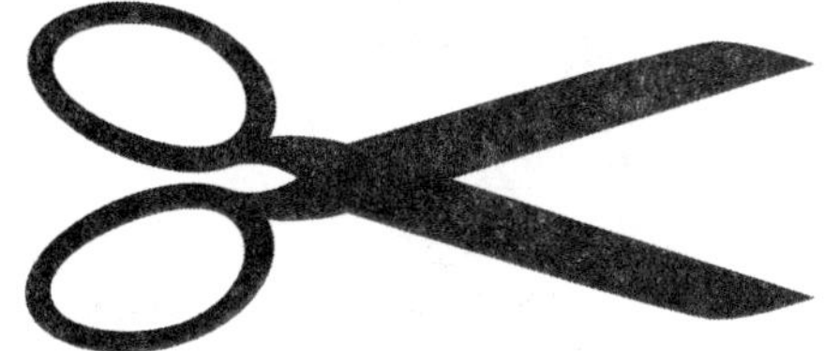

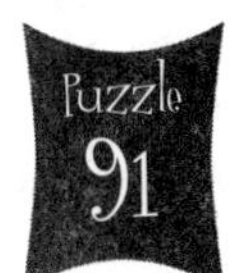

Cut and Glue

Puzzle 91

Cut out the words at the bottom of this page and glue them where they belong to correctly complete Luke 5:20.

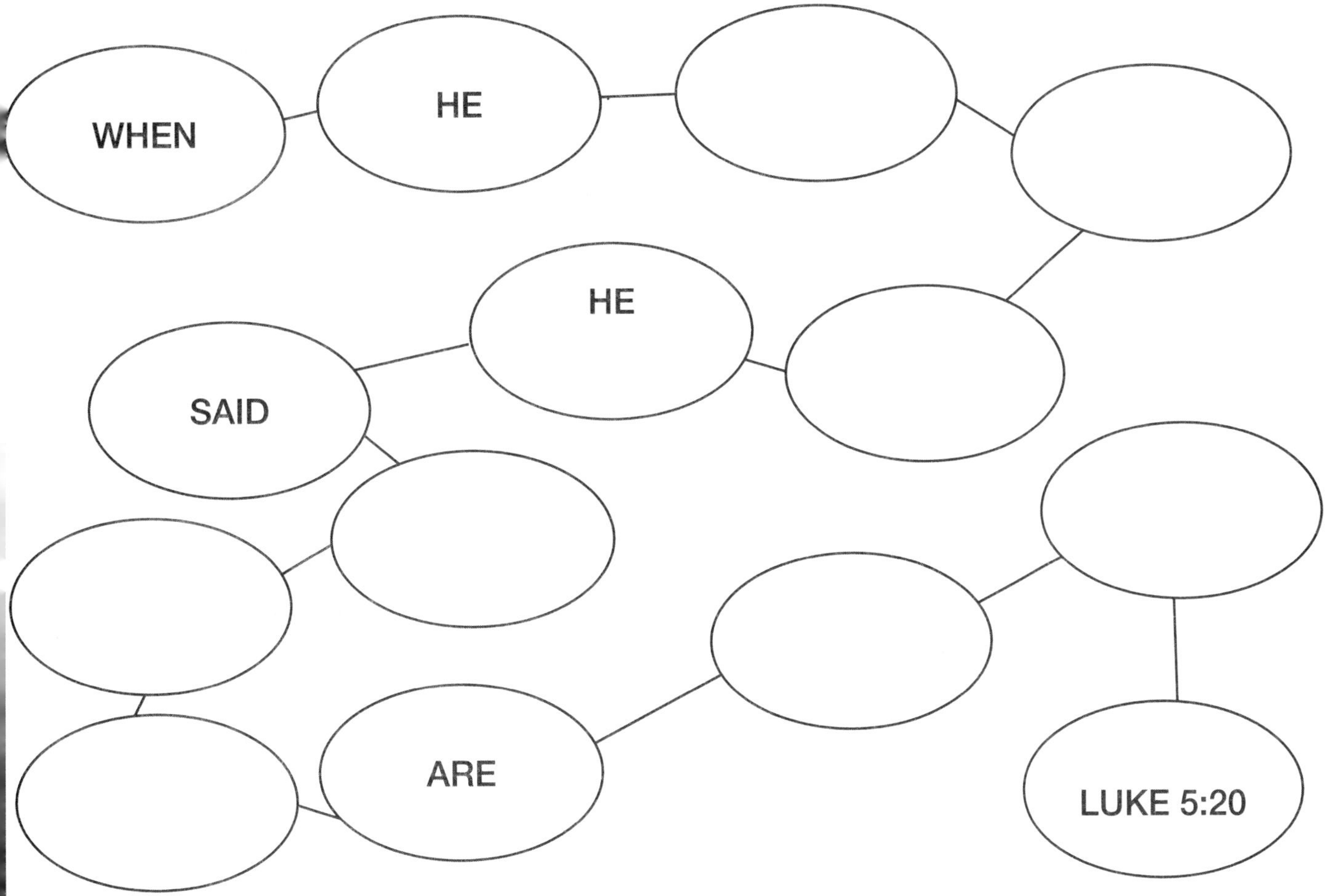
WHEN
HE
HE
SAID
ARE
LUKE 5:20

FAITH

FORGIVEN

THEIR

FRIEND

YOUR

YOU

SAW

SINS

Friends Word Search

In Luke 5:17-26, some friends brought a man who was paralyzed to Jesus to be healed. In the word search below, can you find the words that come from the story? You might want to check the Scripture.

T	G	N	S	P	Y	P	N	L	P	B	B	P	A	S
F	D	N	E	A	H	W	O	A	H	V	T	U	U	V
S	I	W	V	V	O	A	R	W	A	F	O	D	T	U
S	W	V	O	D	I	A	R	V	E	Y	C	N	H	I
K	P	D	T	R	L	G	O	I	A	R	U	A	O	O
Q	E	E	L	Y	C	K	R	V	S	J	D	T	R	L
R	L	P	Z	W	A	L	K	O	L	E	J	S	I	U
U	Z	E	F	R	I	E	N	D	F	E	E	T	T	D
J	D	P	E	X	C	B	V	T	S	H	N	S	Y	R
H	S	T	R	A	E	H	V	U	E	G	E	V	B	O
D	N	V	Z	A	D	L	S	E	F	R	W	A	H	L
H	E	Y	L	D	V	M	Y	A	A	U	B	T	L	R
P	O	Q	N	Q	N	A	W	B	I	M	A	Q	D	O
S	F	O	W	A	W	E	E	N	T	I	E	Y	M	O
T	N	E	M	E	Z	A	M	A	H	C	L	F	Z	F

AMAZEMENT	HEAL	POWER
AUTHORITY	HEARTS	ROOF
AWE	JESUS	SINS
CROWD	LET [. . .] DOWN	STAND UP
FAITH	LORD	WALK
FORGIVEN	PARALYZED	
FRIEND	PHARISEES	

Summer Sunday School Puzzles, © 2008 Abingdon Press

Famous Bible Families

Below are some famous Bible families. One name needs to be added to each family group. Choose from the people listed on the right to fill in the blank for each family on the left.

1. Adam, Eve, Cain, and _______________

2. Abraham, Sarah, and _______________

3. Jacob, Rachel, Leah, and _______________

4. Joseph, Benjamin, and _______________

5. Moses, Miriam, and _______________

6. Ruth, Naomi, and _______________

7. David, Bathsheba, Solomon, and _______________

8. Joseph, Mary, and _______________

9. Elizabeth, Zechariah, and _______________

10. Mary, Martha, and _______________

11. Timothy, Lois, and _______________

Aaron

Abel

Absalom

Boaz

Eunice

Isaac

Jesus

John the Baptist

Judah

Laban

Lazarus

MISSING VOWELS

Somebody left the vowels out of our Bible verse. Can you figure out where they go? (The vowels are *AEIOU*; for this puzzle, *Y* will be a consonant). We've put the vowels in a box for you so you can know how many of each you can use.

A A A A A A A A A A   E E E E E E E E E E E E

I I I I I I I I I I I I I I I   O O O O O O O O O O

U U U U U U

__ __ __M __R __M __ND __D __F Y__ __R

S __NC__R__ F __ __TH, __ F __ __TH TH __T

L__V __D F __RST __N Y__ __R GR __NDM __TH __R

L __ __S __ND Y__ __R M __TH __R __ __N __C __

__ND N __W, __ __M S __R __, L __V __S __N

Y__ __ __. 2 T__ M __ THY 1:5

It's Your Move

Start at the outlined box and move from box to box across, down, or diagonally to find a Bible verse. Every box will be used once. All letters are in the right order. If you can't figure it out, just read Psalm 46:1.

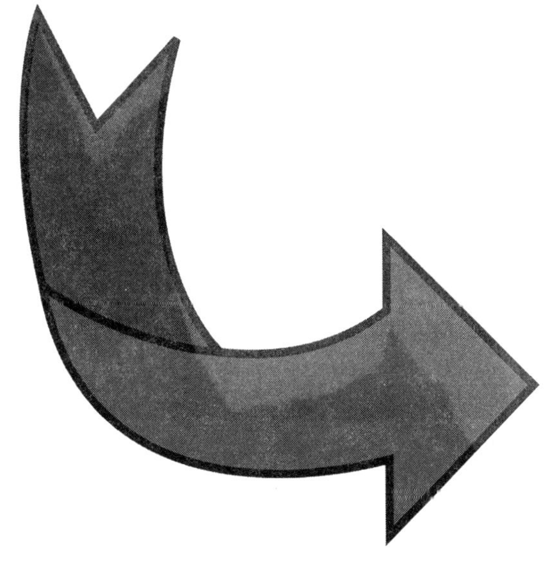

ST	AND	FUGE	OUR
GTH	REN	RE	IS
A	VERY	**GOD**	BLE
ES	PR	IN	OU
ENT	HE	LP	TR

EXTRA ALPHABET LETTERS

OOPS! Each set of alphabet letters has one extra letter. Write the extra letter on the line to the right of the alphabet. When you read down, you will discover what 1 Kings 18:39b says.

ABCDEFGHIJKLMNOPQRSTTUVWXYZ ◄············► ☐

ABCDEFGHHIJKLMNOPQRSTUVWXYZ ◄············► ☐

ABCDEEFGHIJKLMNOPQRSTUVWXYZ ◄············► ☐

ABCDEFGHIJKLLMNOPQRSTUVWXYZ ◄············► ☐

ABCDEFGHIJKLMNOOPQRSTUVWXYZ ◄············► ☐

ABCDEFGHIJKLMNOPQRRSTUVWXYZ ◄············► ☐

ABCDDEFGHIJKLMNOPQRSTUVWXYZ ◄············► ☐

ABCDEFGHIIJKLMNOPQRSTUVWXYZ ◄············► ☐

ABCDEFGHIJKLMNNOPQRSTUVWXYZ ◄············► ☐

ABCDDEFGHIJKLMNOPQRSTUVWXYZ ◄············► ☐

ABCDEEFGHIJKLMNOPQRSTUVWXYZ ◄············► ☐

ABCDEEFGHIJKLMNOPQRSTUVWXYZ ◄············► ☐

ABCDDEFGHIJKLMNOPQRSTUVWXYZ ◄············► ☐

ABCDEFGHIIJKLMNOPQRSTUVWXYZ ◄············► ☐

ABCDEFGHIJKLMNOPQRSSTUVWXYZ ◄············► ☐

ABCDEFGGHIJKLMNOPQRSTUVWXYZ ◄············► ☐

ABCDEFGHIJKLMNOOPQRSTUVWXYZ ◄············► ☐

ABCDDEFGHIJKLMNOPQRSTUVWXYZ ◄············► ☐

The Healing of Naaman

Based on 2 Kings 5:1-19

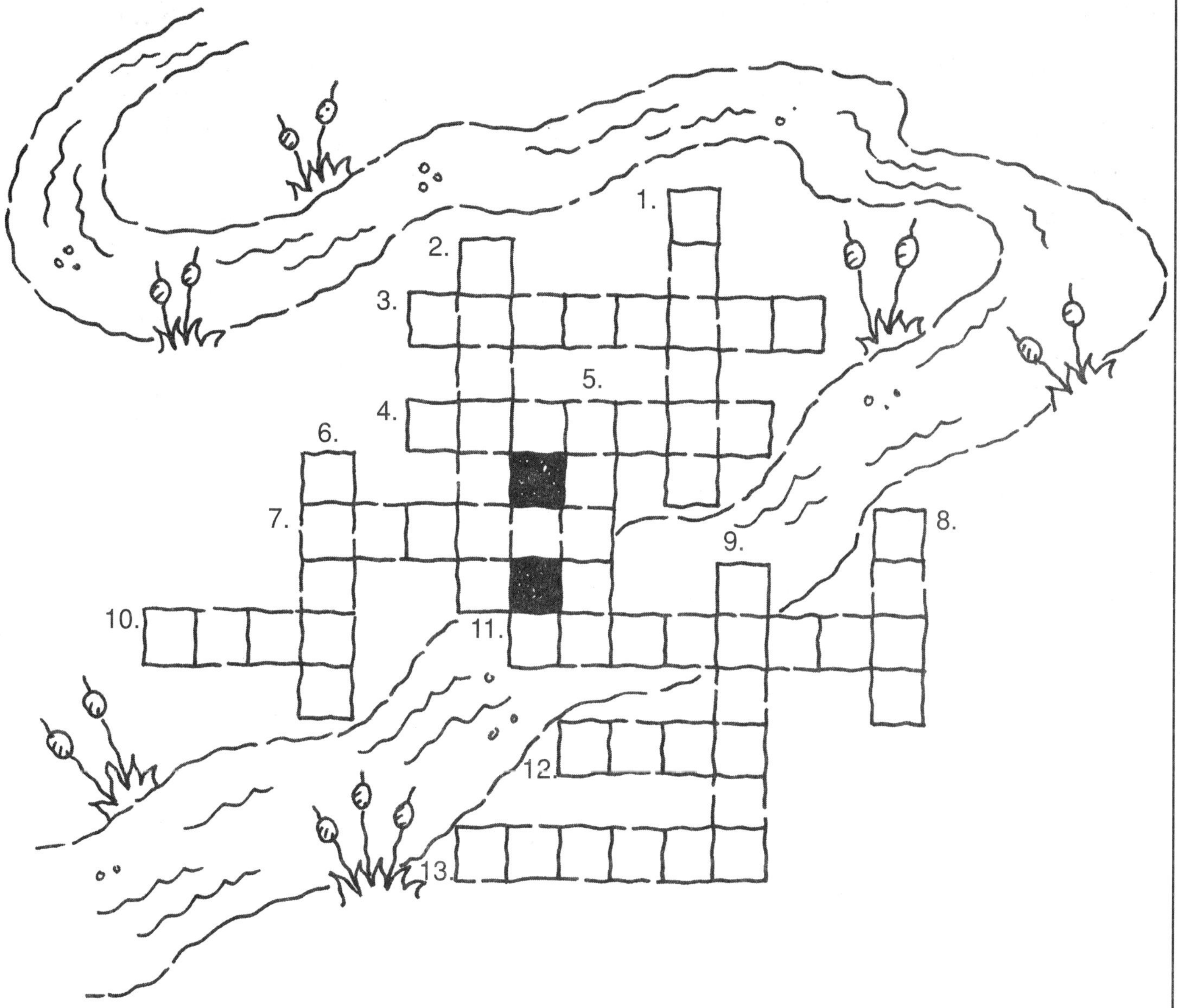

ACROSS

3. to become clean again (verse 14)
4. one who speaks for God (verse 8)
7. name of prophet (verse 8)
10. what Naaman wants (verse 7)
11. people who work for other people (verse 13)
12. where Naaman is from (verse 5)
13. the name of the river (verse 10)

DOWN

1. Where does Naaman go? (verse 5)
2. Naaman's disease (verse 1)
5. Naaman was told to leave in this way. (verse 19)
6. the number of times Naaman was dipped (verse 10)
8. to become clean (verse 10)
9. main character of the story (verse 1)

What Is It?

Read the clues on the puzzle pieces below to try to figure out why Naaman couldn't pay Elisha for the miracle of healing.

Summer Sunday School Puzzles, © 2008 Abingdon Press

Circle to Circle

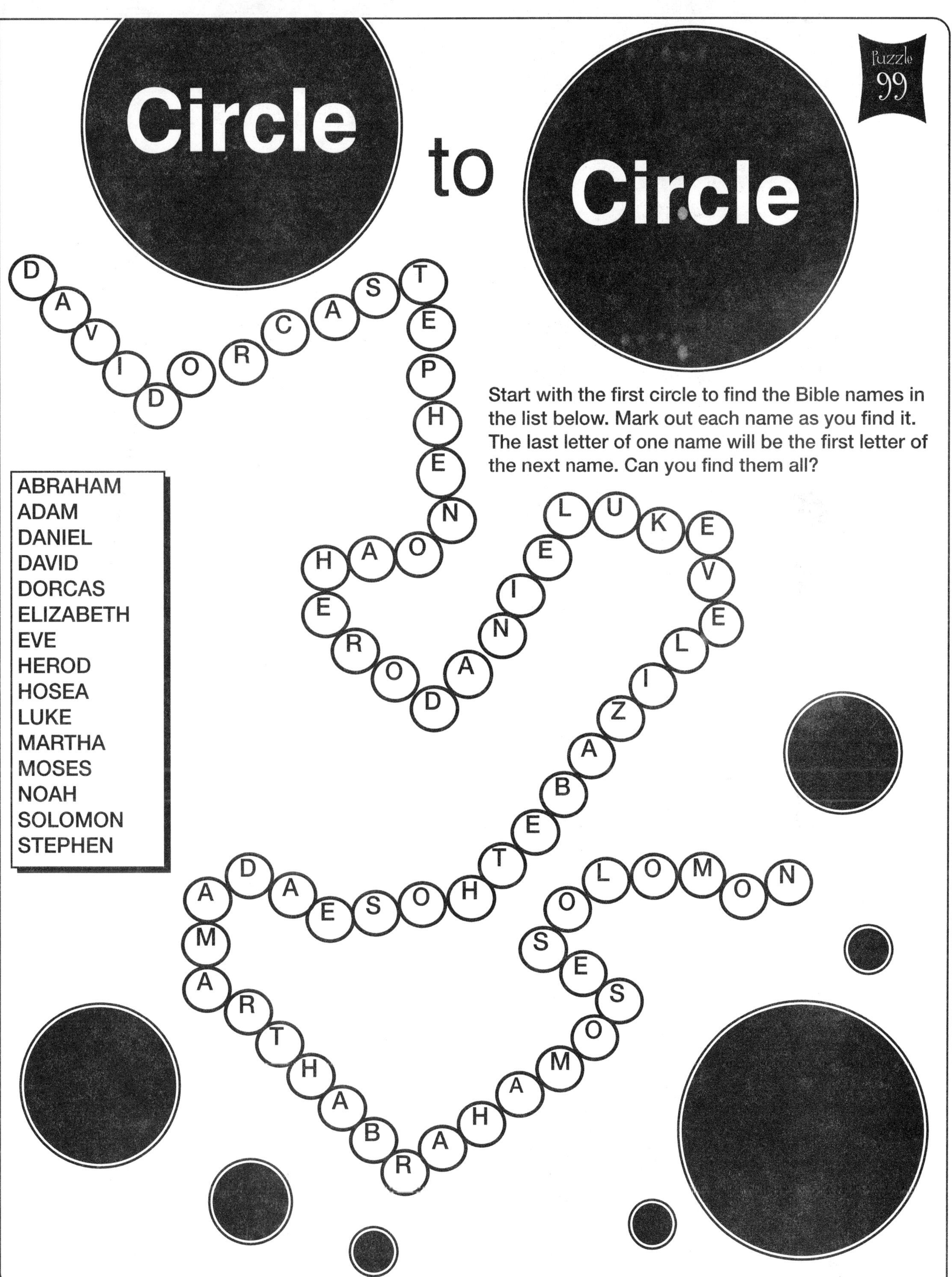

Start with the first circle to find the Bible names in the list below. Mark out each name as you find it. The last letter of one name will be the first letter of the next name. Can you find them all?

ABRAHAM
ADAM
DANIEL
DAVID
DORCAS
ELIZABETH
EVE
HEROD
HOSEA
LUKE
MARTHA
MOSES
NOAH
SOLOMON
STEPHEN

Puzzle 100

DROP THE Zs

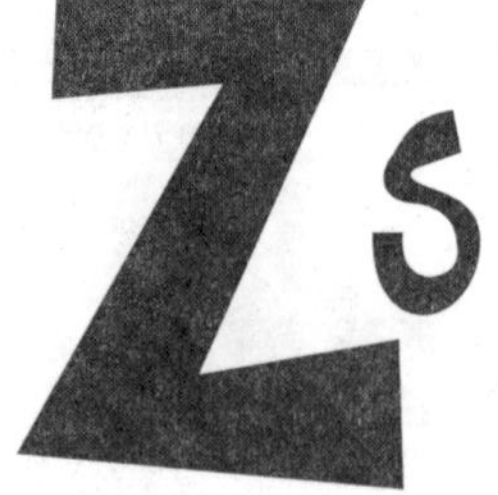

Mark out all of the Zs below and you will be able to read John 14:1.

ZZDOZZZNOTZZLETZZZZYOURZHEZARTSZZ

ZZZBEZZZTROZZUBZLEDZZZZ.

ZBELIZZEVEZZINZZZGODZZZZ,

ZZZBEZLIEZVEZZALZSOZZZINZMZEZZ.

Healing the Sick

There are many stories in the Bible of Jesus healing the sick.
Match the people who were ill with what Jesus did to cure them.

BY LETTER AND NUMBER

Substitute the correct letter for the number and discover what Hebrews 11:1 tells us.

A	=	26
B	=	25
C	=	24
D	=	23
E	=	22
F	=	21
G	=	20
H	=	19
I	=	18
J	=	17
K	=	16
L	=	15
M	=	14
N	=	13
O	=	12
P	=	11
Q	=	10
R	=	9
S	=	8
T	=	7
U	=	6
V	=	5
W	=	4
X	=	3
Y	=	2
Z	=	1

```
___  ___  ___      ___  ___  ___  ___  ___      ___  ___
 13   12   4        21   26   18   7    19        18   8

___  ___  ___      ___  ___  ___  ___  ___  ___  ___  ___  ___
 7    19   22       26   8    8    6    9    26   13   24   22

___  ___      ___  ___  ___  ___  ___  ___
 12   21       7    19   18   13   20   8

___  ___  ___  ___  ___      ___  ___  ___ ,     ___  ___  ___
 19   12   11   22   23       21   12   9        7    19   22

___  ___  ___  ___  ___  ___  ___  ___  ___  ___      ___  ___
 24   12   13   5    18   24   7    18   12   13       12   21

___  ___  ___  ___  ___  ___      ___  ___  ___
 7    19   18   13   20   8        13   12   7

___  ___  ___  ___ .
 8    22   22   13
```

MIRACLE MAZE

Puzzle 103

Jesus performed many miracles, and this maze shows us five of them. Find your way through the maze. What are the five miracles? What do they tell us about Jesus?

How Many?

Solve the math problems to discover the answers to the questions.

After his resurrection, Jesus appeared to some disciples who were fishing.

How many disciples were there?

Add these together to get the answer:
Simon Peter + Thomas + Nathanael,
+ the 2 sons of Zebedee, + 2 other disciples = _______ .

How far were they from land when they began dragging the net?

25 x 2 + 60 - 10 = _______________ yards off shore.

How many fish did they catch because of the instructions Jesus gave them?

277 - 155 + 35 - 4 = _______________ fish.

Jesus had appeared to the disciples before. What number was this appearance to the disciples after Jesus' resurrection?

33 divided by 3 - 8 = __________. It was the __________ time that Jesus appeared to the disciples after he was raised from the dead.

Check your answers in John 21:1-14.

   Summer Sunday School Puzzles, © 2008 Abingdon Press

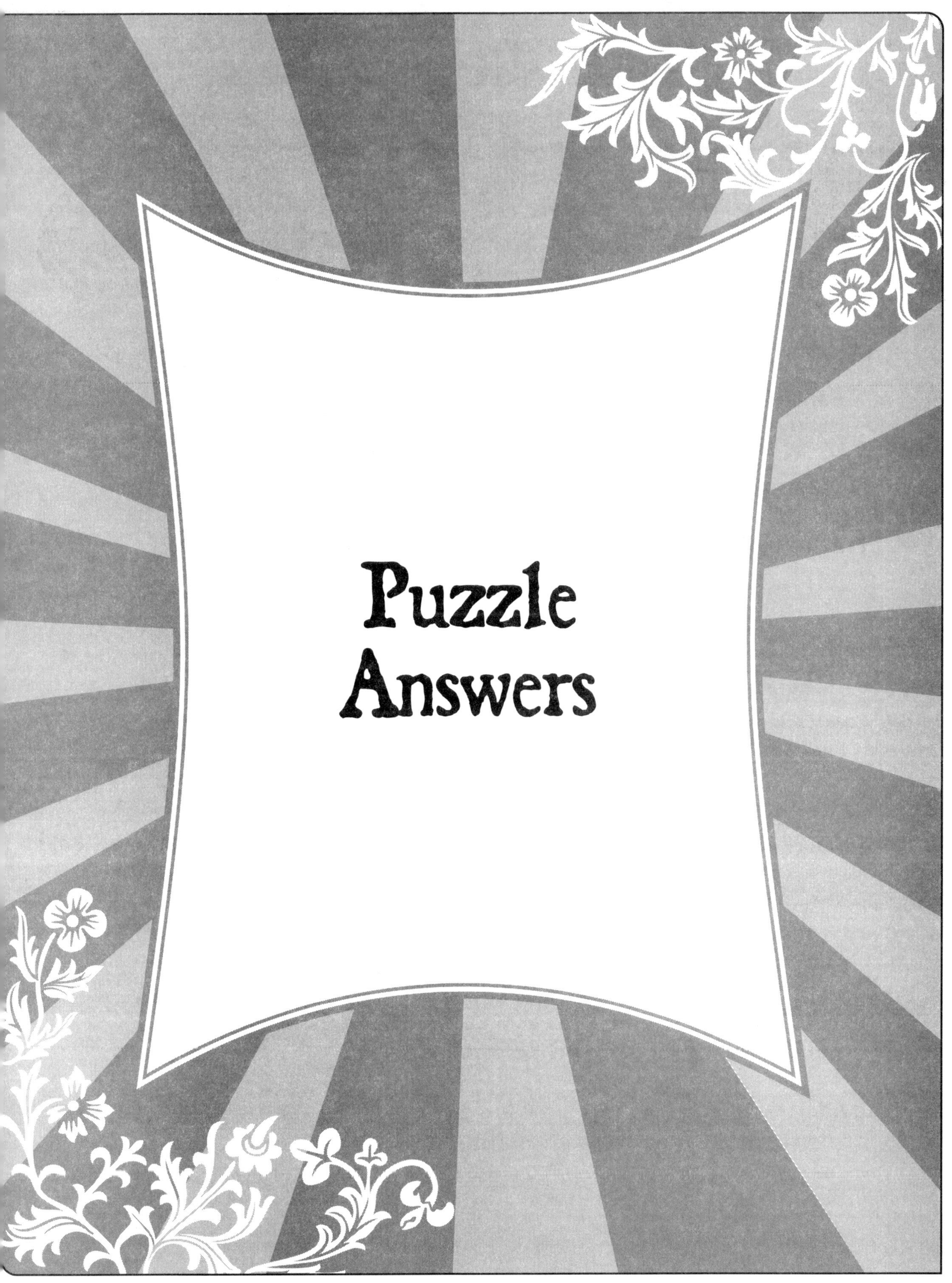

Puzzle
Answers

Puzzle 1

C R E A T E D I N G O D S I M A G E

Puzzle 2

Puzzle 3

NOAH WAS A RIGHTEOUS MAN, BLAMELESS IN HIS GENERATION; NOAH WALKED WITH GOD.

Puzzle 4

1. cypress wood
2. rooms
3. pitch
4. three hundred cubits
5. fifty cubits
6. thirty cubits
7. roof
8. a cubit above
9. in its side
(AT BOTTOM: three: lower, second, and third)

Puzzle 5

I have made you the ancestor of a multitude of nations

Puzzle 6

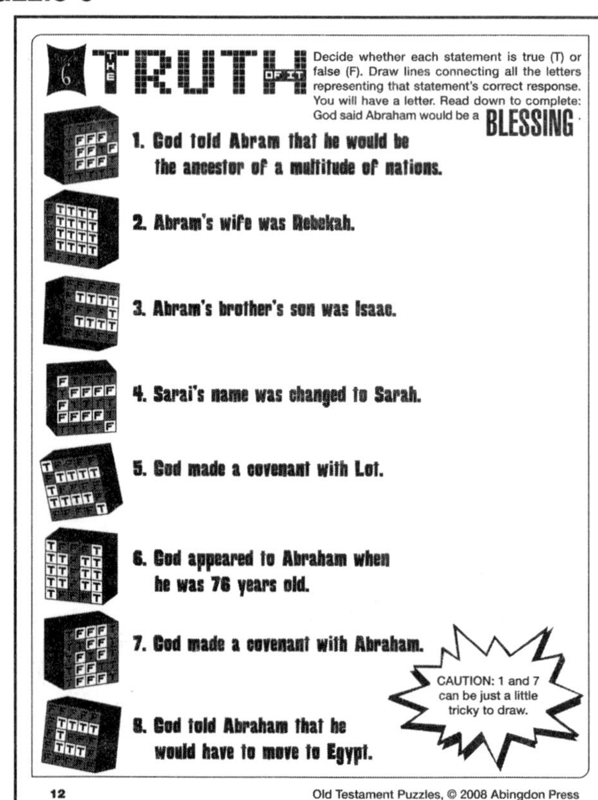

Puzzle Answers

Puzzle 7

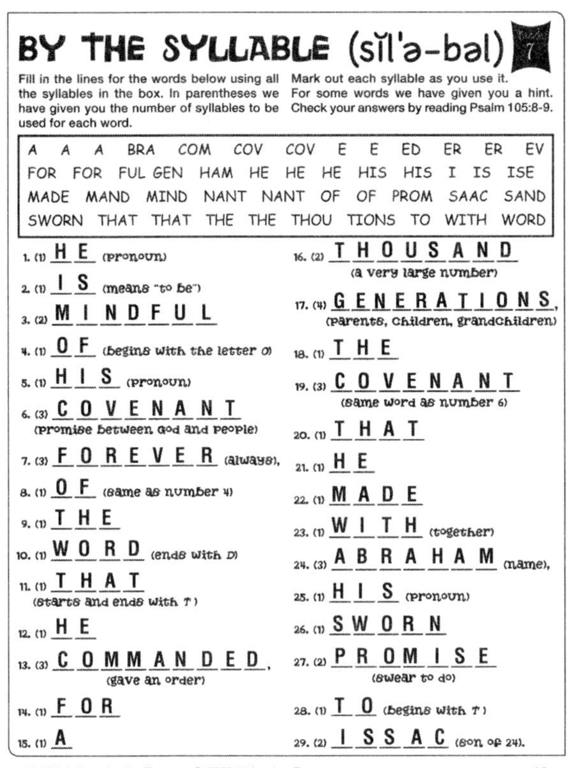

Puzzle 9

Puzzle 8

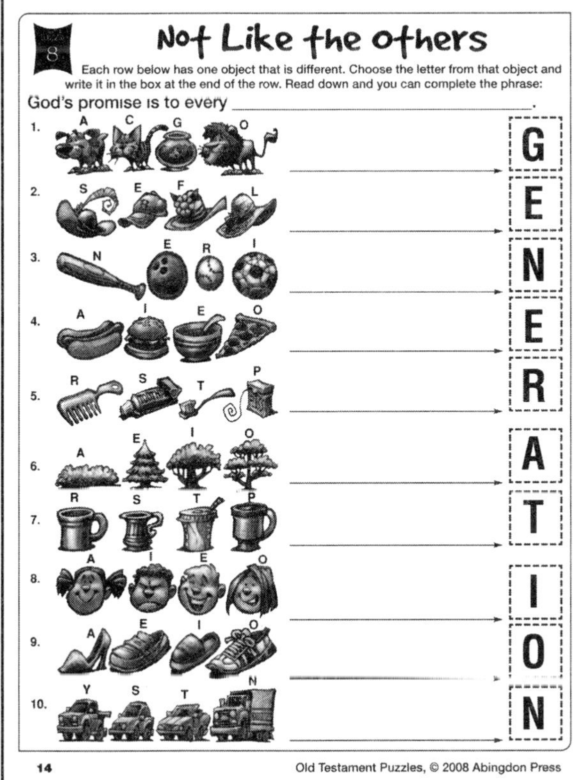

Puzzle 10

Puzzle 11

Puzzle 12

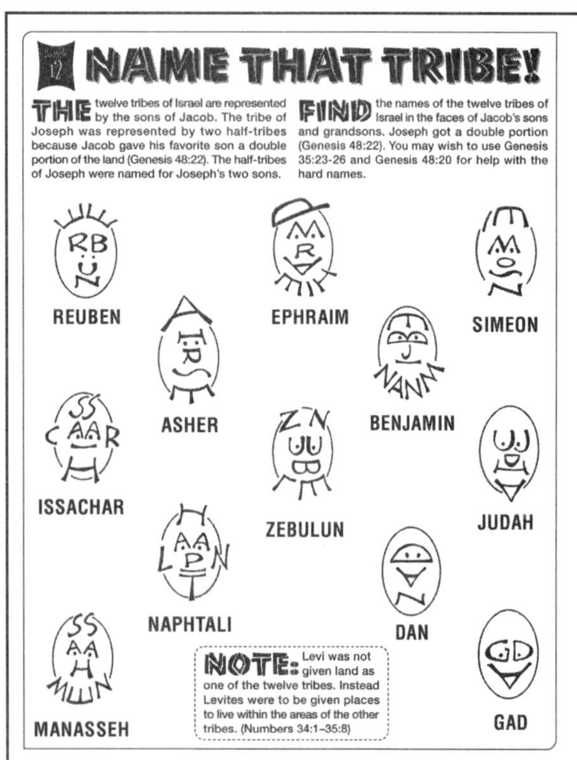

Puzzle 13

Work	Kill	Drink
Word	Sill	Drank
Ward	Silt	Prank
Lard	Salt	Plank
Land	Sale	Plane
	Save	Place

Puzzle 14

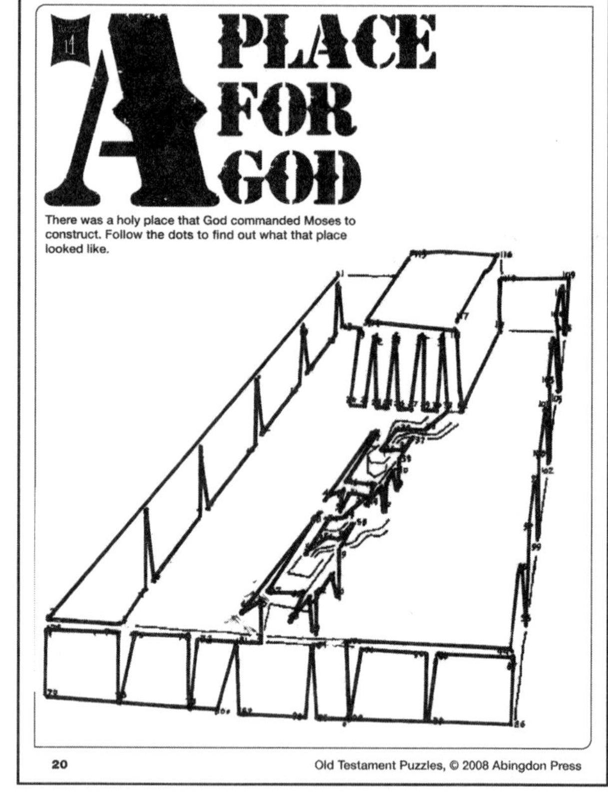

Puzzle 15

Choose this day whom you will serve, . . . but as for me and my household, we will serve the LORD.

Puzzle 16

BE STRONG
AND COURAGEOUS
DO NOT BE
FRIGHTENED OR
DISMAYED, FOR
THE LORD YOUR
GOD IS WITH
YOU WHEREVER
YOU GO.

Puzzle 17:

1. We	6. work	11. love
2. know	7. together	12. God
3. that	8. for	13. purpose
4. all	9. those	
5. things	10. who	

Puzzle 18:

Scrambled letters: D O L E S S B L R
Unscrambled: B L E S S [the] L O R D

Puzzle 19:

```
G          G
O          O
D          D
I          S
S          I
K          T
I          S
N          O
G          N
O          H
V          I
E          S
R          H
T          O
H          L
E          Y
N          T
A          H
T          R
I          O
O          N
N          E
S
```

Puzzle 20:

6, 11, 1, 9, 5, 2, 13, 7, 14, 8, 3, 10, 12, 4
(Based on 1 Samuel 8–31.)

Puzzle 21:

Be **strong**, be **courageous**, and **keep** the **charge** of the LORD your God, **walking** in his **ways** and **keeping** his **statutes**, his **commandments**, his **ordinances**, and his **testimonies**.

Puzzle 22

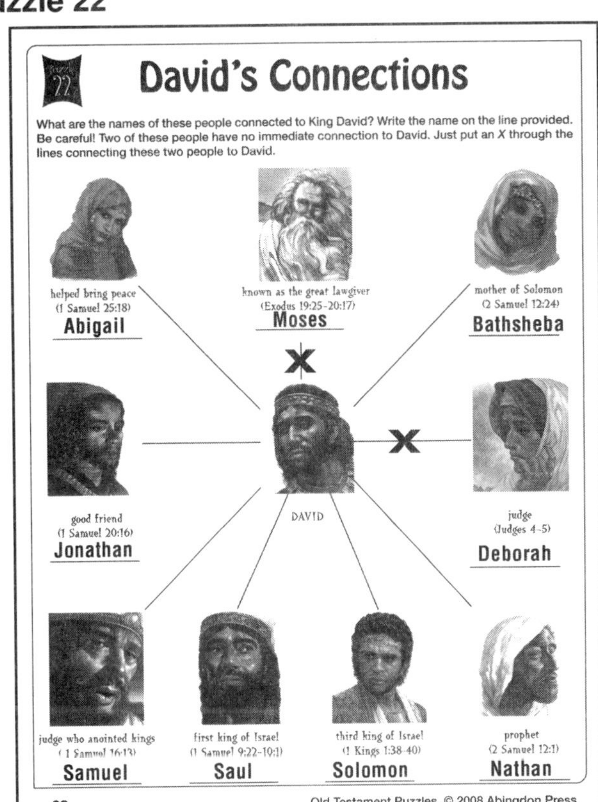

Puzzle 23:

GOD IS OUR REFUGE AND STRENGTH, A VERY PRESENT HELP IN TROUBLE.

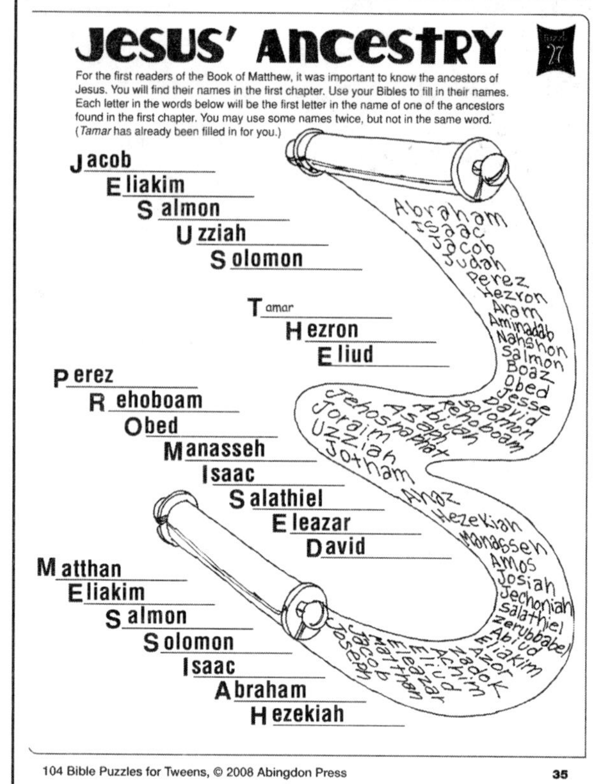

Puzzle 25:

I WILL RAISE UP FOR
DAVID A RIGHTEOUS
BRANCH.

Puzzle 26:

THE DAYS
ARE SURELY COMING SAYS
THE LORD WHEN I WILL RAISE
UP FOR DAVID A RIGHTEOUS
BRANCH AND HE SHALL REIGN
AS KING AND DEAL WISELY AND
SHALL EXECUTE JUSTICE AND
RIGHTEOUSNESS IN THE LAND

Puzzle 28
1. ABRAHAM
2. SARAH
3. ISAAC
4. ISRAEL
5. ESAU
6. JOSEPH
7. MOSES
8. JOSHUA
9. DEBORAH
10. KING SAUL
11. DAVID
12. SOLOMON
13. DIVIDED KINGDOM
14. PROPHETS
15. MARY
EVERY GENERATION

Puzzle 29

magnifies
servant
now on
thoughts
thrones
ancestors
descendants
remained
magnificat

Puzzle 31

Puzzle 30

Puzzle 32

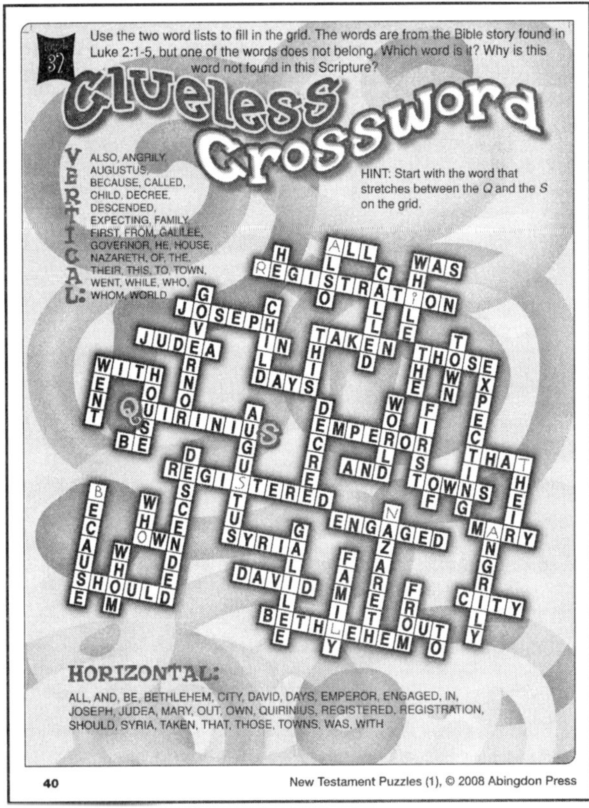

Which word is it? ANGRILY

Why is this word not found in Scripture?
THIS QUESTION IS FOR DISCUSSION.

Puzzle 33

Puzzle 34

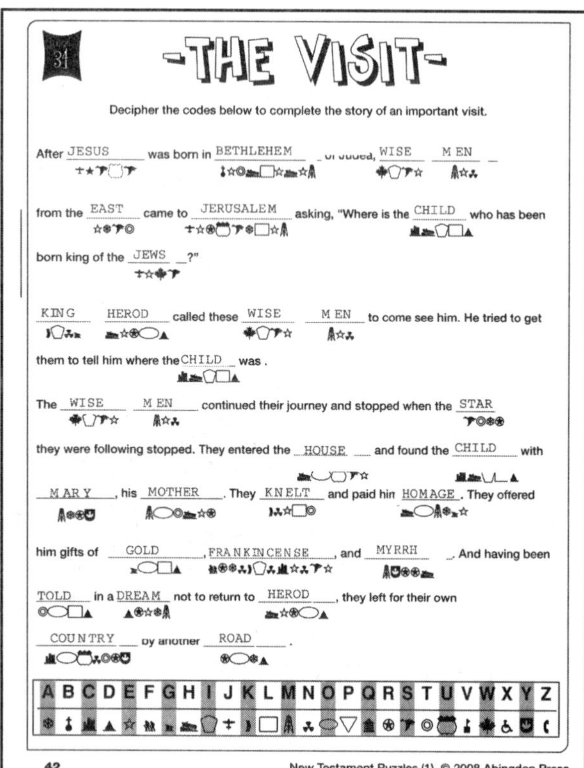

Puzzle 35:

1. S
2. A
3. C
4. R
5. A
6. M
7. E
8. N
9. T

Puzzle 36:

1. THIS
2. IS
3. MY
4. SON
5. THE
6. BELOVED
7. WITH
8. WHOM
9. I
10. AM
11. WELL
12. PLEASED

Puzzle 37:

FOLLOW ME AND I WILL MAKE YOU FISH FOR PEOPLE.

Puzzle 38

Puzzle 39

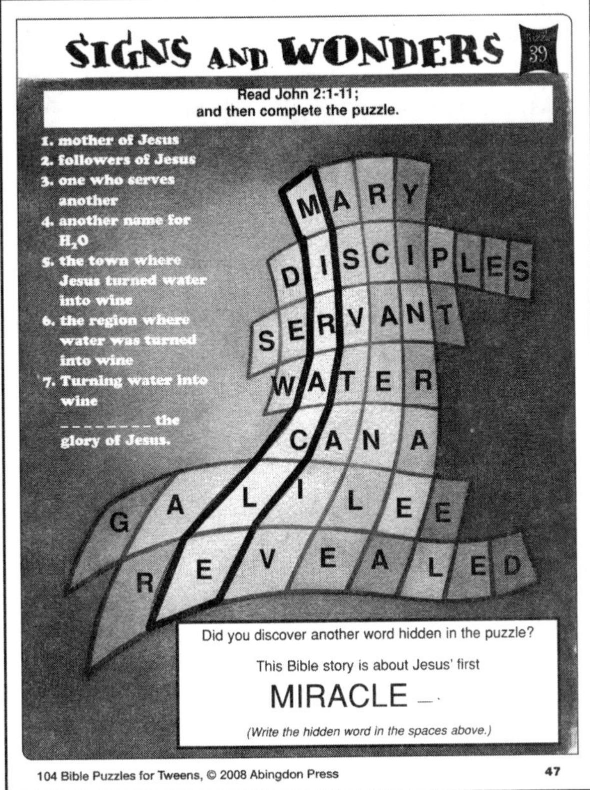

Puzzle 40

F
F
T
T
T
F

Puzzle 41

B   A wise child makes a glad father, but a foolish child is a mother's grief. **Proverbs 10:1**

S   Beware of false prophets, who come to you in sheep's clothing but inwardly are ravenous wolves. **Matthew 7:15**

S   Blessed are the poor in spirit, for theirs is the kingdom of heaven. **Matthew 5:3**

B   Do not boast about tomorrow, for you do not know what a day may bring.
Proverbs 27:1

O   I destroy my enemy when I make him my friend. **Abraham Lincoln**

S   If you forgive others their trespasses, your heavenly Father will also forgive you.
Matthew 6:14

(continued in next column)

(Puzzle 41 continued)

S   In everything do to others as you would have them do to you. **Matthew 7:12**

O   It is better to deserve honors and not have them than to have them and not deserve them. **Mark Twain (Samuel Clemens)**

S   Let your light shine before others, so that they may see your good works and give glory to your Father in heaven. **Matthew 5:16**

B   Love is patient; love is kind; love is not envious or boastful or arrogant or rude.
1 Corinthians 13:4-5a

S   Love your enemies and pray for those who persecute you. **Matthew 5:44**

S   No one can serve two masters.
Matthew 6:24

B   Owe no one anything. **Romans 13:8a**

O   Whatever is begun in anger ends in shame. **Benjamin Franklin**

O   When anger rises, think of the consequences. **K'ung-fu-tzu (Confucius)**

S   For where your treasure is, there your heart will be also. **Matthew 6:21**

O   You cannot shake hands with a clenched fist. **Indira Gandhi**

Puzzle 42

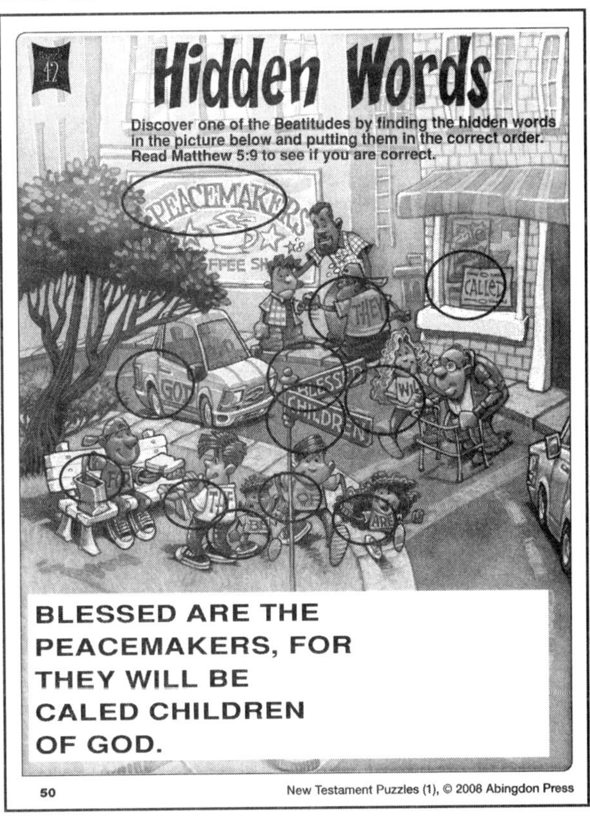

Puzzle 43

WE HAD TO
CELEBRATE
AND REJOICE,
BECAUSE
THIS BROTHER
OF YOURS WAS
DEAD AND HAS
COME TO LIFE;
HE WAS LOST AND
HAS BEEN FOUND.

Puzzle 45

Puzzle 44

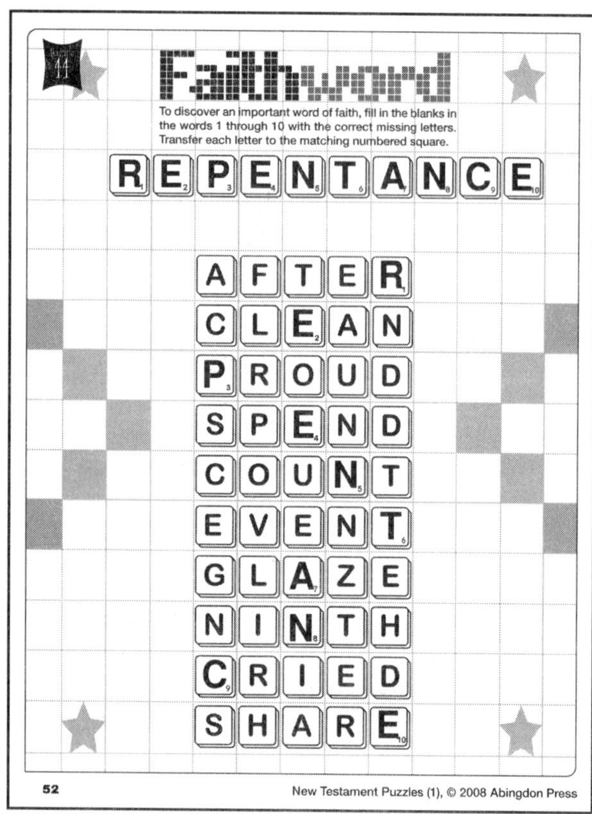

Puzzle 46

Puzzle 47

Puzzle 49

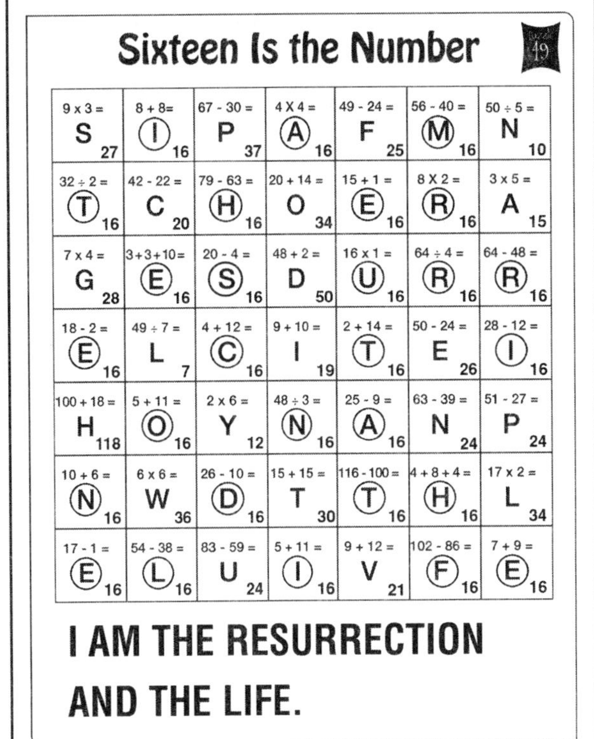

Sixteen Is the Number

9 x 3 =	8 + 8 =	67 - 30 =	4 X 4 =	49 - 24 =	56 - 40 =	50 ÷ 5 =
S 27	I 16	P 37	A 16	F 25	M 16	N 10
32 ÷ 2 =	42 - 22 =	79 - 63 =	20 + 14 =	15 + 1 =	8 X 2 =	3 x 5 =
T 16	C 20	H 16	O 34	E 16	R 16	A 15
7 x 4 =	3 + 3 + 10 =	20 - 4 =	48 + 2 =	16 x 1 =	64 ÷ 4 =	64 - 48 =
G 28	E 16	S 16	D 50	U 16	R 16	R 16
18 - 2 =	49 ÷ 7 =	4 + 12 =	9 + 10 =	2 + 14 =	50 - 24 =	28 - 12 =
E 16	L 7	C 16	I 19	T 16	E 26	I 16
100 + 18 =	5 + 11 =	2 x 6 =	48 ÷ 3 =	25 - 9 =	63 - 39 =	51 - 27 =
H 118	O 16	Y 12	N 16	A 16	N 24	P 24
10 + 6 =	6 x 6 =	26 - 10 =	15 + 15 =	116 - 100 =	4 + 8 + 4 =	17 x 2 =
N 16	W 36	D 16	T 30	T 16	H 16	L 34
17 - 1 =	54 - 38 =	83 - 59 =	5 + 11 =	9 + 12 =	102 - 86 =	7 + 9 =
E 16	L 16	U 24	I 16	V 21	F 16	E 16

I AM THE RESURRECTION
AND THE LIFE.

Puzzle 48

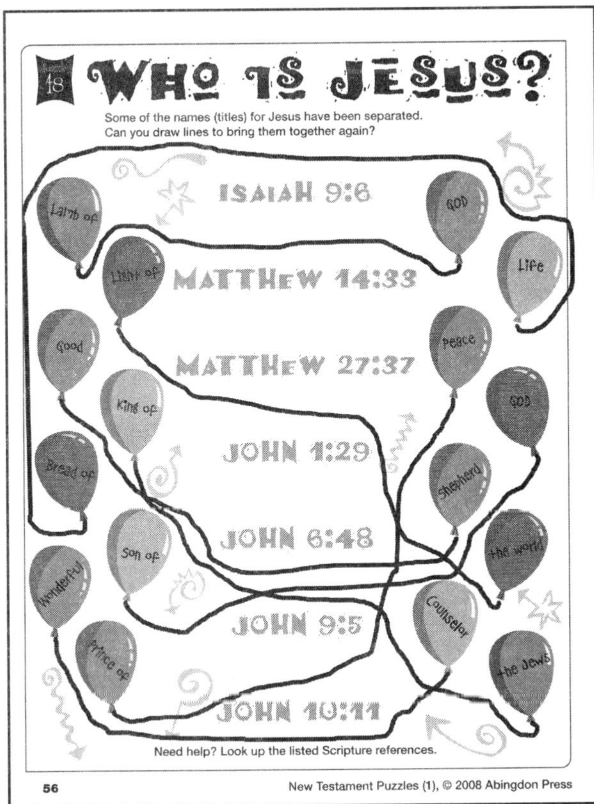

Puzzle 50

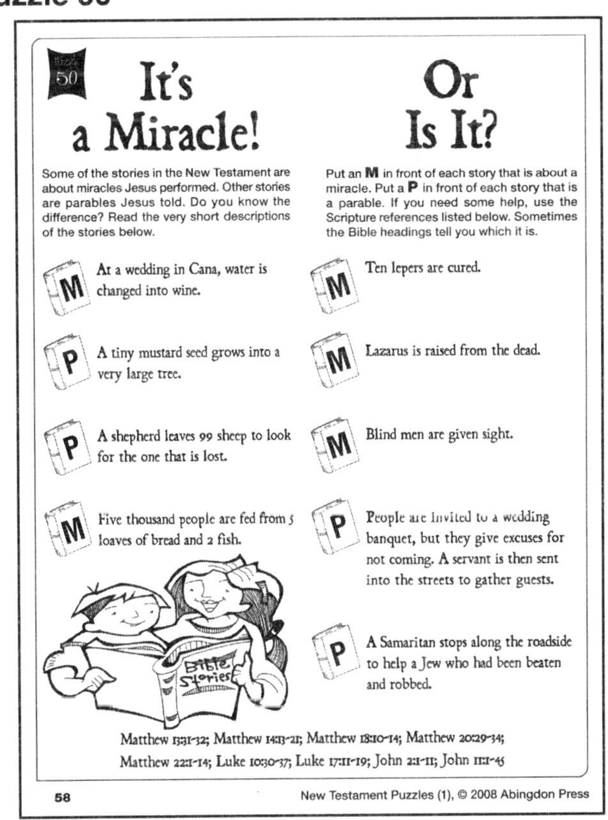

It's a Miracle!   Or Is It?

Some of the stories in the New Testament are about miracles Jesus performed. Other stories are parables Jesus told. Do you know the difference? Read the very short descriptions of the stories below.

Put an **M** in front of each story that is about a miracle. Put a **P** in front of each story that is a parable. If you need some help, use the Scripture references listed below. Sometimes the Bible headings tell you which it is.

M At a wedding in Cana, water is changed into wine.

P A tiny mustard seed grows into a very large tree.

P A shepherd leaves 99 sheep to look for the one that is lost.

M Five thousand people are fed from 5 loaves of bread and 2 fish.

M Ten lepers are cured.

M Lazarus is raised from the dead.

M Blind men are given sight.

P People are invited to a wedding banquet, but they give excuses for not coming. A servant is then sent into the streets to gather guests.

P A Samaritan stops along the roadside to help a Jew who had been beaten and robbed.

Matthew 13:31-32; Matthew 14:13-21; Matthew 18:10-14; Matthew 20:29-34; Matthew 22:1-14; Luke 10:30-37; Luke 17:11-19; John 2:1-11; John 11:1-45

Puzzle 51

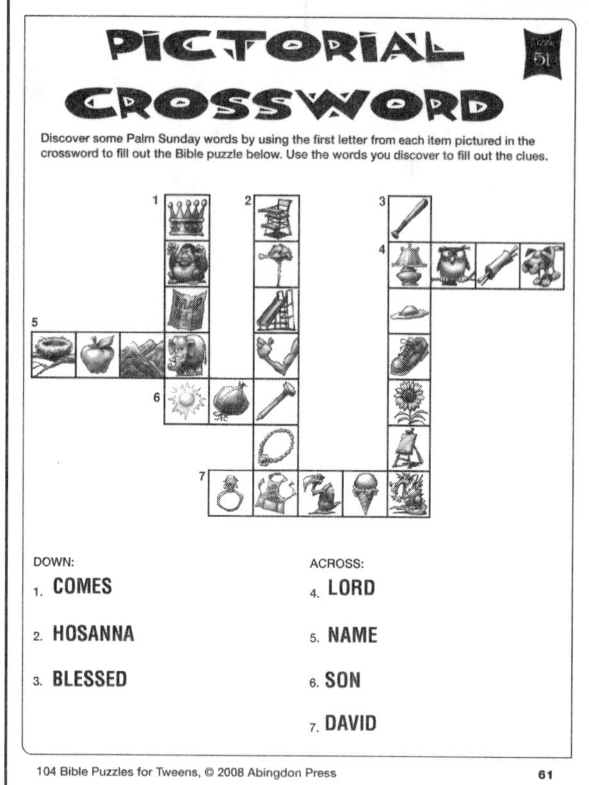

Puzzle 52

THIS IS THE PROPHET JESUS FROM NAZARETH IN GALILEE.

Puzzle 53

BUT STRIVE FIRST FOR THE KINGDOM OF GOD AND HIS RIGHTEOUSNESS AND ALL THESE THINGS WILL BE GIVEN TO YOU AS WELL

Puzzle 54

Luke 2:8-15—angels—shepherds—find Savior

Matthew 2:1-11—star led—wise men—find king

Matthew 4:18-22—Jesus—Simon Peter, Andrew, James, and John—follow Jesus/fish for people

Luke 19:1-6—Jesus—Zacchaeus—Come down; I must stay at your house.
(continued in next column)

(Puzzle 54 continued)
Luke 10:1-9—Jesus—disciples—cure sick; tell people about kingdom of God

Mark 16:15-16—Jesus—disciples—proclaim good news to world

Puzzle 55

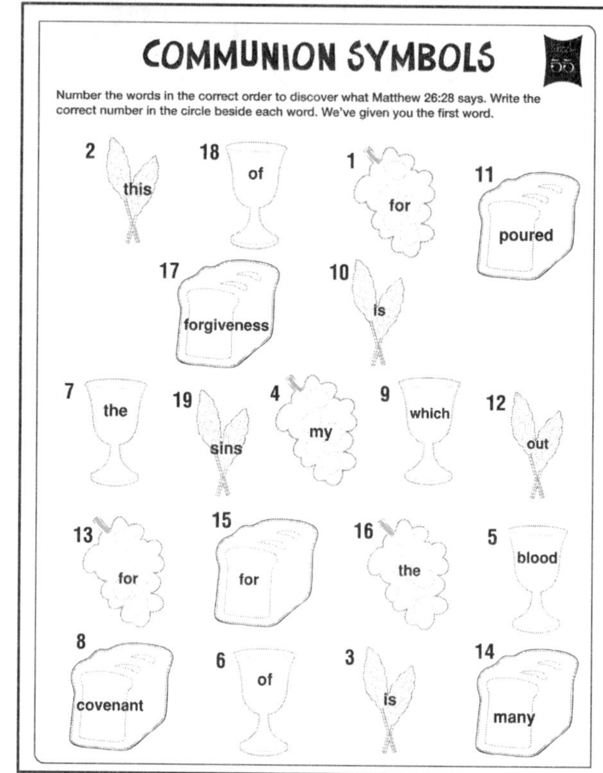

Puzzle 56

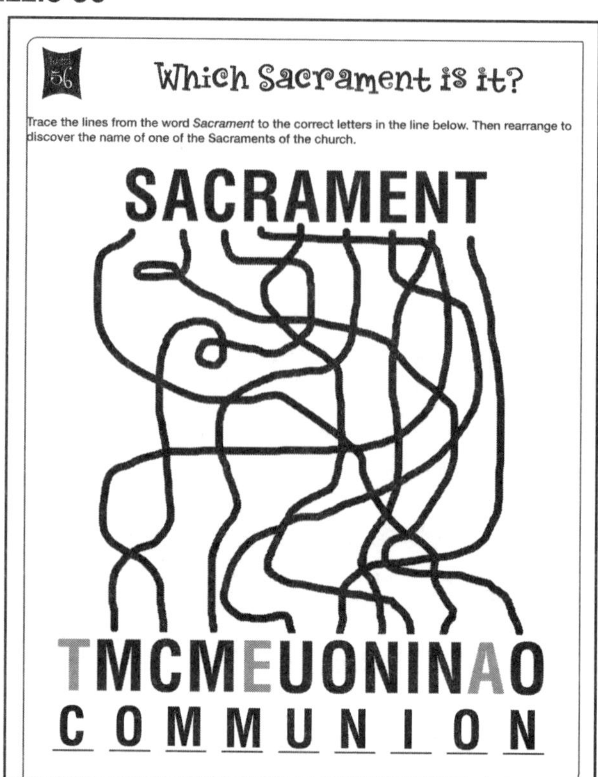

Puzzle Answers

Puzzle 57

Puzzle 59

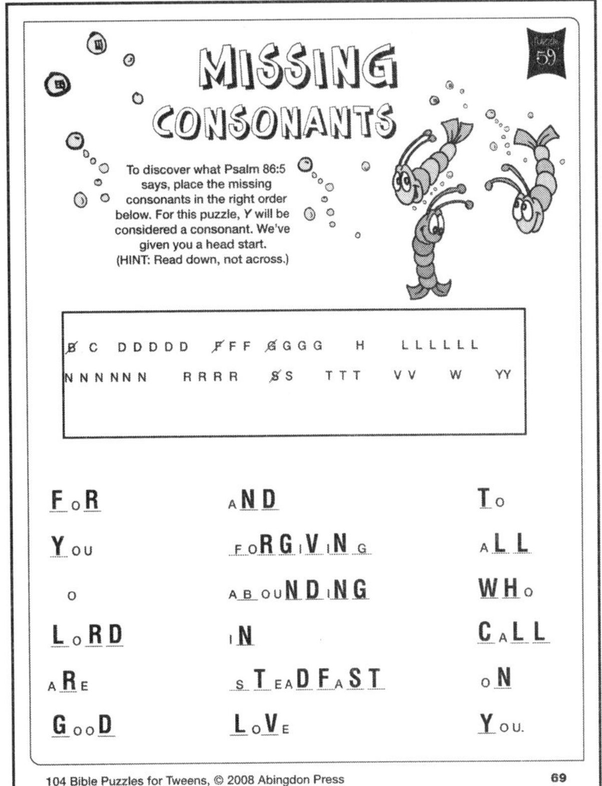

Puzzle 58

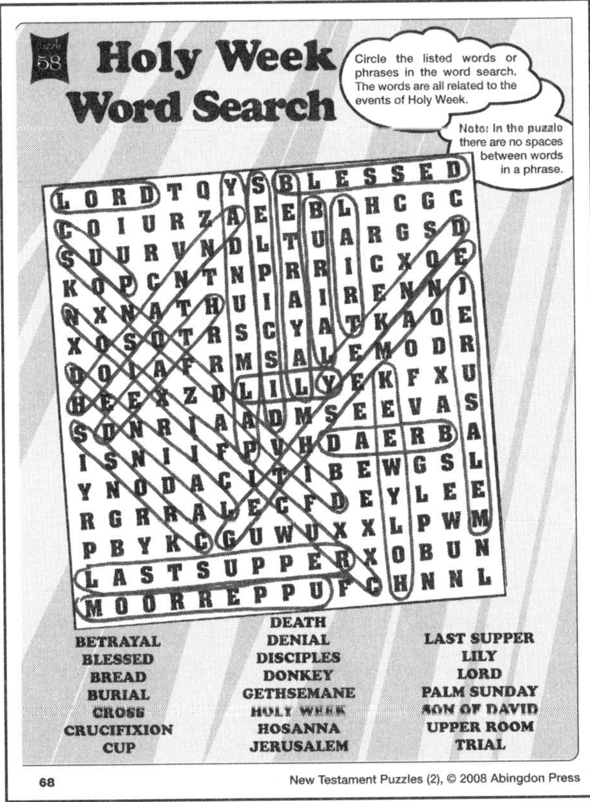

Puzzle 60

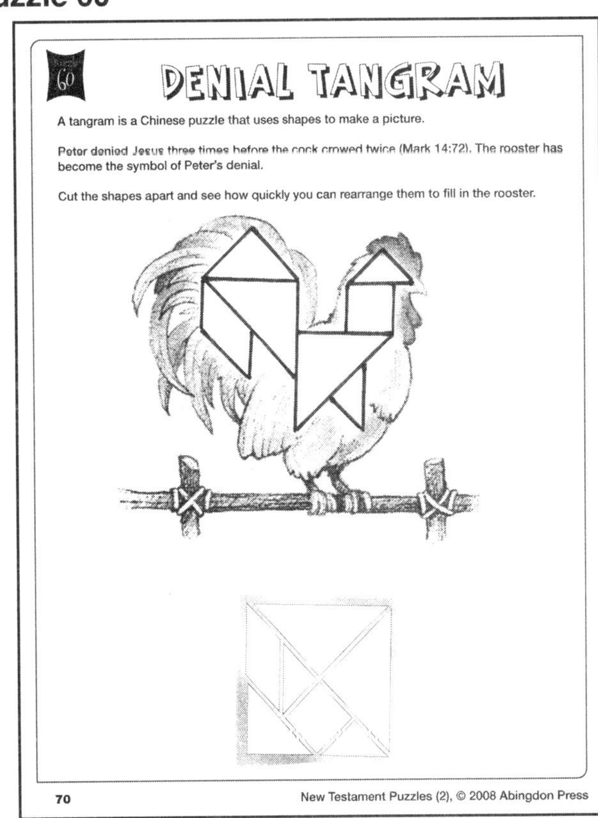

Puzzle 61:

1. Truly
2. this
3. man
4. was
5. God's
6. son

Puzzle 62

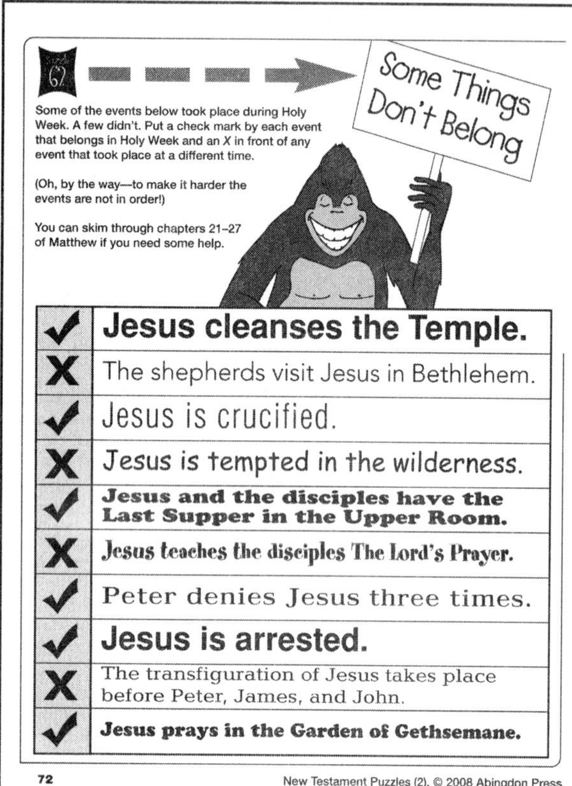

Puzzle 63

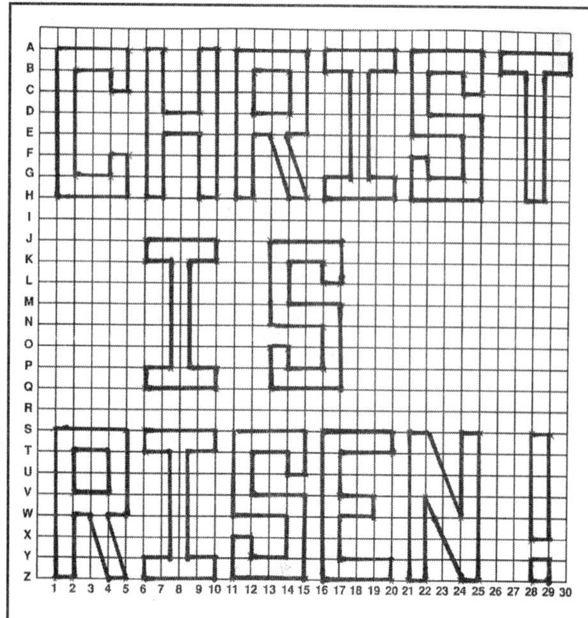

Puzzle 64

RESURRECTION

Puzzle 65

GO THEREFORE AND MAKE DISCIPLES OF ALL NATIONS BAPTIZING THEM IN THE NAME OF THE FATHER AND OF THE SON AND OF THE HOLY SPIRIT AND TEACHING THEM TO OBEY EVERYTHING THAT I HAVE COMMANDED YOU. MATTHEW 28:19-20

Puzzle 66

by the breaking of the bread

Puzzle 67

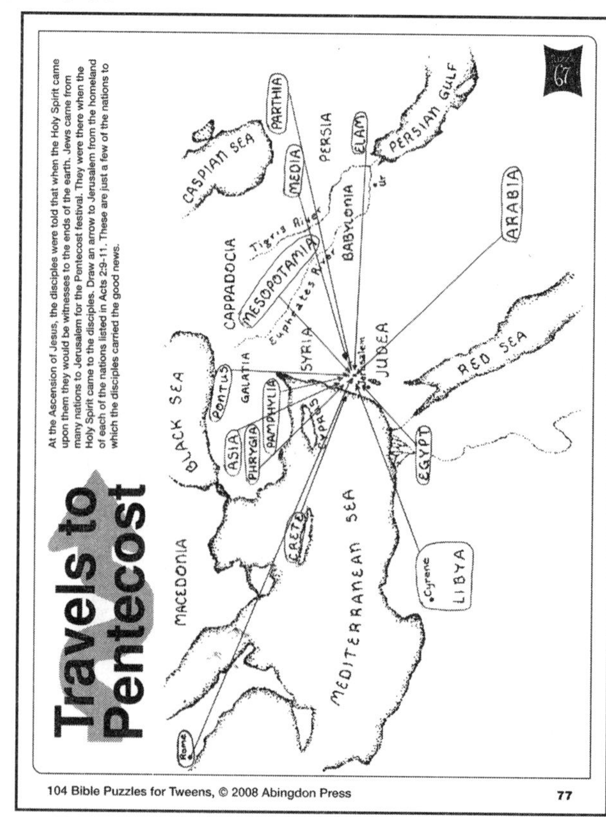

Puzzle 68

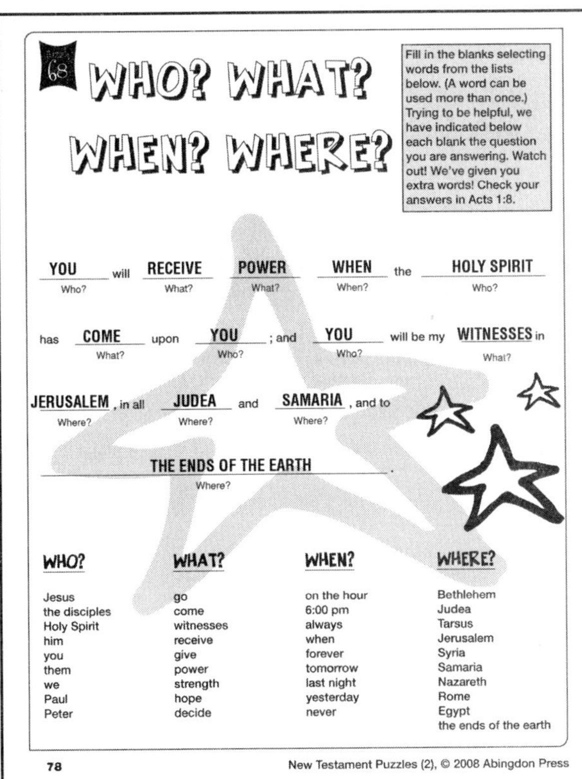

New Testament Puzzles (2), © 2008 Abingdon Press

Puzzle 69

ASI	ACYR	ENE	= Asia, Cyrene
PEN	TEC	OST	= Pentecost
MED	ESLI	BYA	= Medes, Libya
JUD	EAEG	YPT	= Judea, Egypt
GALI	LEA	NS	= Galileans
ELA	MIT	ESG OD	= Elamites, God
MESO	POT	AMIA	= Mesopotamia
PAM	PHY	LIA	= Pamphylia
HOL	YSPI	RIT	= Holy Spirit
JER	USA	LEM	= Jerusalem
JE	WSCR	ETANS	= Jews, Cretans
PAR	THI	ANS	= Parthians
PON	TUSR	OME	= Pontus, Rome
PHR	YGIAJ	EWS	= Phrygia, Jews
SPIR	ITAR	ABS	= Spirit, Arabs
CAPP	ADO	CIA	= Cappadocia

Puzzle 70

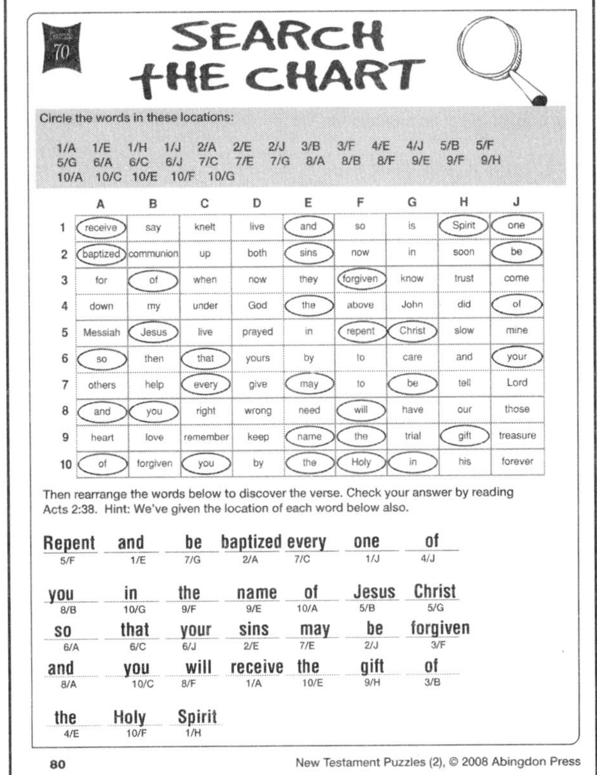

	A	B	C	D	E	F	G	H	J
1	receive	say	knelt	live	and	so	is	Spirit	one
2	baptized	communion	up	both	sins	now	in	soon	be
3	for	of	when	now	they	forgiven	know	trust	come
4	down	my	under	God	the	above	John	did	of
5	Messiah	Jesus	live	prayed	in	repent	Christ	slow	mine
6	so	then	that	yours	by	to	care	and	your
7	others	help	every	give	may	to	be	tell	Lord
8	and	you	right	wrong	need	will	have	our	those
9	heart	love	remember	keep	name	the	trial	gift	treasure
10	of	forgiven	you	by	the	Holy	in	his	forever

Then rearrange the words below to discover the verse. Check your answer by reading Acts 2:38. Hint: We've given the location of each word below also.

Repent	and	be	baptized	every	one	of
5/F	1/E	7/G	2/A	7/C	1/J	4/J

you	in	the	name	of	Jesus	Christ
8/B	10/G	9/F	9/E	10/A	5/B	5/G

so	that	your	sins	may	be	forgiven
6/A	6/C	6/J	2/E	7/E	2/J	3/F

and	you	will	receive	the	gift	of
8/A	10/C	8/F	1/A	10/E	9/H	3/B

the	Holy	Spirit				
4/E	10/F	1/H				

80   New Testament Puzzles (2), © 2008 Abingdon Press

Puzzle 71

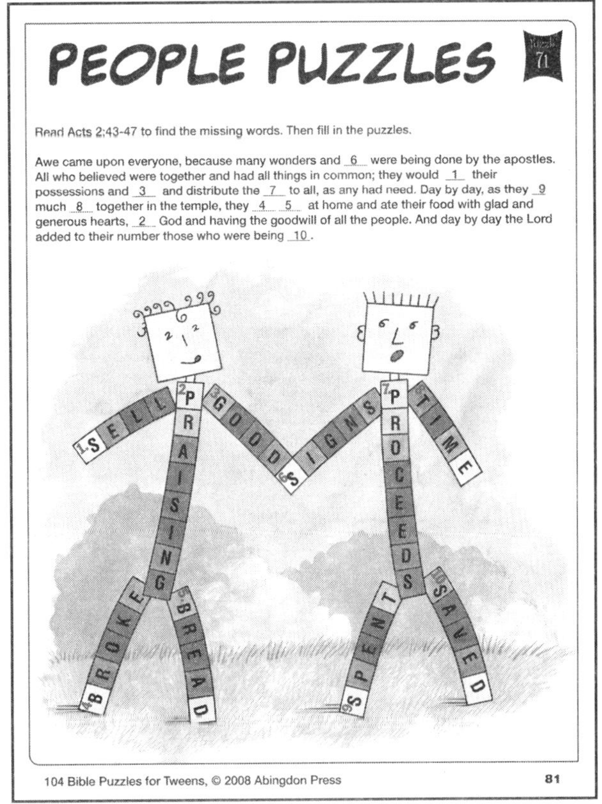

104 Bible Puzzles for Tweens, © 2008 Abingdon Press   81

Puzzle 72

teaching, fellowship, breaking of bread, prayers

Puzzle 73

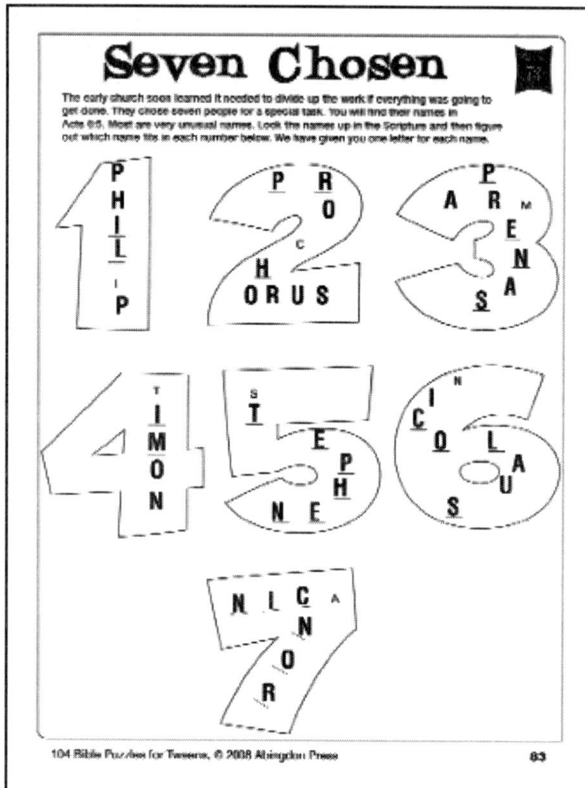

Puzzle 74

Now there are varieties of gifts, but the same Spirit; and there are varieties of services, but the same Lord; and there are varieties of activities, but it is the same God who activates all of them in everyone. To each is given the manifestation of the Spirit for the common good.

Puzzle 75

I have fought the good fight, I have finished the race, I have kept the faith.

Puzzle 76

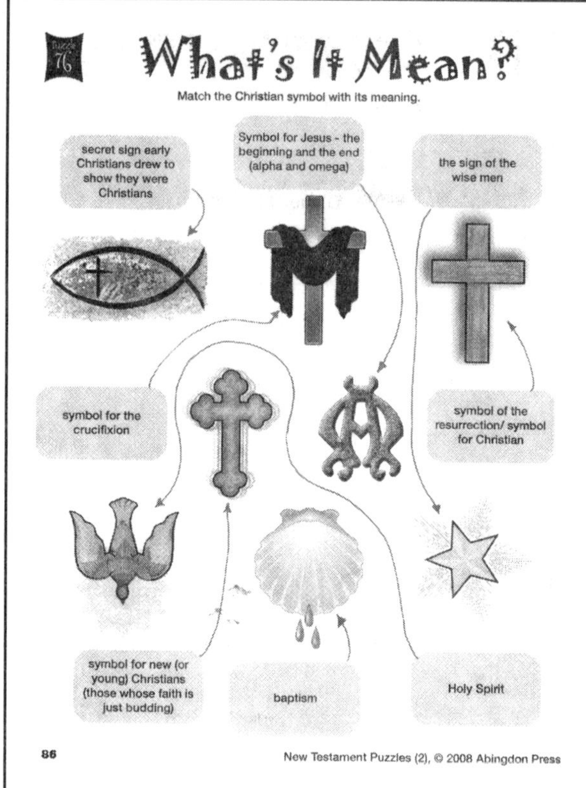

Puzzle 77

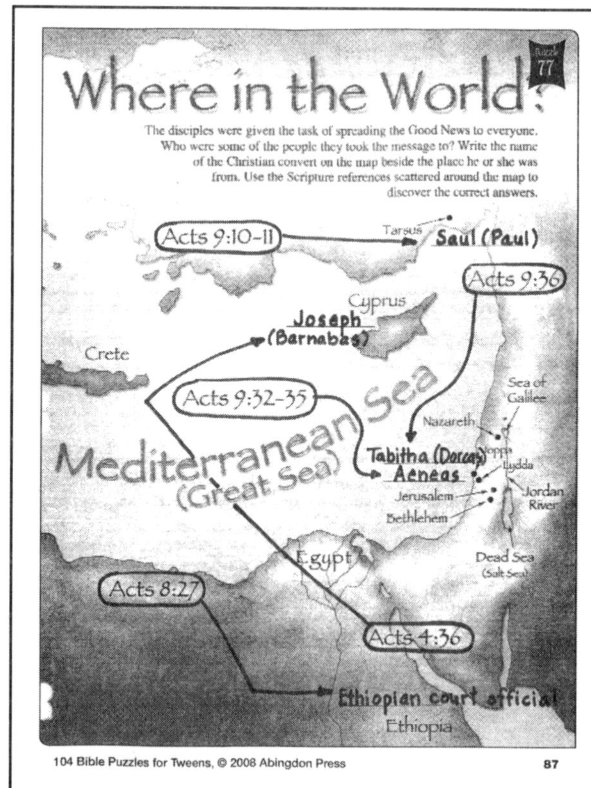

Puzzle Answers

Puzzle 78

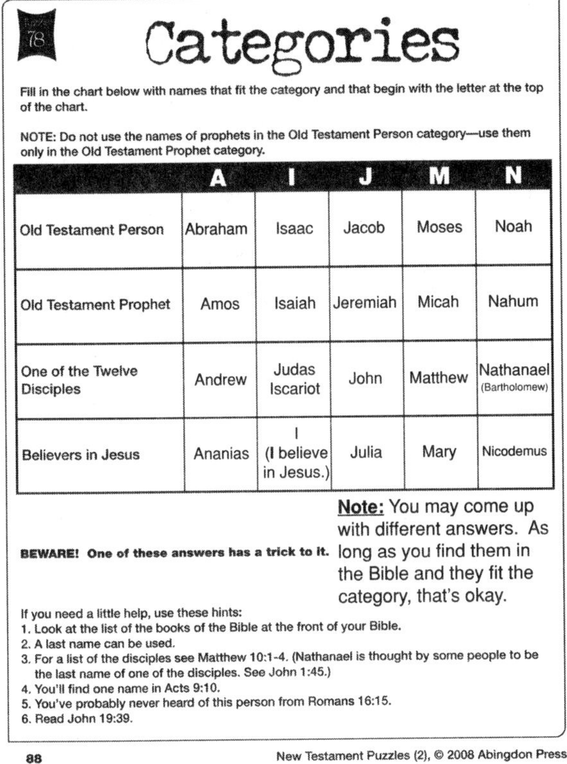

Categories

Fill in the chart below with names that fit the category and that begin with the letter at the top of the chart.

NOTE: Do not use the names of prophets in the Old Testament Person category—use them only in the Old Testament Prophet category.

	A	I	J	M	N
Old Testament Person	Abraham	Isaac	Jacob	Moses	Noah
Old Testament Prophet	Amos	Isaiah	Jeremiah	Micah	Nahum
One of the Twelve Disciples	Andrew	Judas Iscariot	John	Matthew	Nathanael (Bartholomew)
Believers in Jesus	Ananias	I (I believe in Jesus.)	Julia	Mary	Nicodemus

Note: You may come up with different answers. As long as you find them in the Bible and they fit the category, that's okay.

BEWARE! One of these answers has a trick to it.

If you need a little help, use these hints:
1. Look at the list of the books of the Bible at the front of your Bible.
2. A last name can be used.
3. For a list of the disciples see Matthew 10:1-4. (Nathanael is thought by some people to be the last name of one of the disciples. See John 1:45.)
4. You'll find one name in Acts 9:10.
5. You've probably never heard of this person from Romans 16:15.
6. Read John 19:39.

 New Testament Puzzles (2), © 2008 Abingdon Press

Puzzle 79

O give thanks
to the LORD,
for he is good;
for his steadfast
love endures
forever.
Psalm 107:1

Puzzle 80

Answers will vary.

Puzzle 81

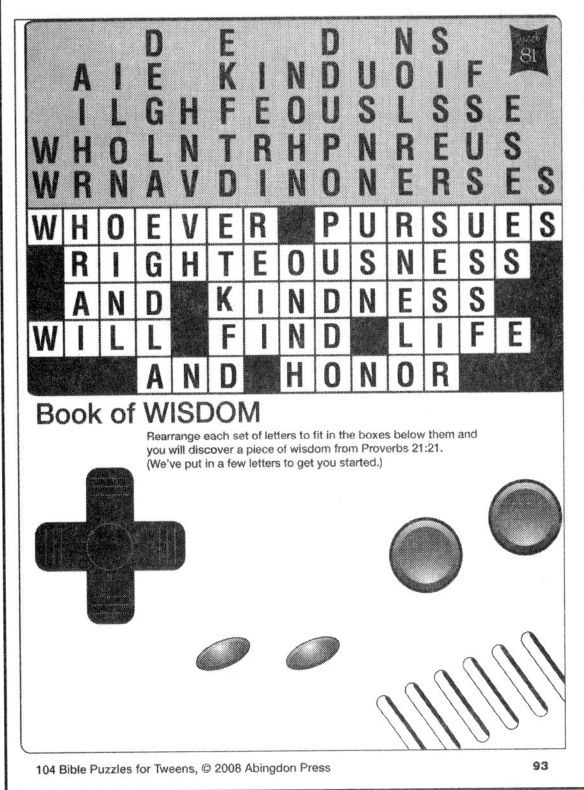

Book of WISDOM

Rearrange each set of letters to fit in the boxes below them and you will discover a piece of wisdom from Proverbs 21:21. (We've put in a few letters to get you started.)

Puzzle 82

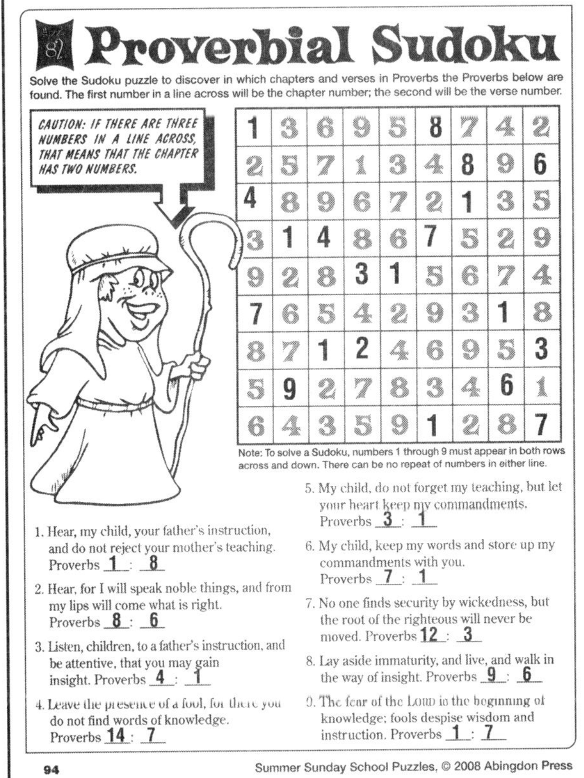

Proverbial Sudoku

Solve the Sudoku puzzle to discover in which chapters and verses in Proverbs the Proverbs below are found. The first number in a line across will be the chapter number; the second will be the verse number.

1	3	6	9	5	8	7	4	2
2	5	7	1	3	4	8	9	6
4	8	9	6	7	2	1	3	5
3	1	4	8	6	7	5	2	9
9	2	8	3	1	5	6	7	4
7	6	5	4	2	9	3	1	8
8	7	1	2	4	6	9	5	3
5	9	2	7	8	3	4	6	1
6	4	3	5	9	1	2	8	7

Note: To solve a Sudoku, numbers 1 through 9 must appear in both rows across and down. There can be no repeat of numbers in either line.

1. Hear, my child, your father's instruction, and do not reject your mother's teaching. Proverbs __1__ : __8__

2. Hear, for I will speak noble things, and from my lips will come what is right. Proverbs __8__ : __6__

3. Listen, children, to a father's instruction, and be attentive, that you may gain insight. Proverbs __4__ : __1__

4. Leave the presence of a fool, for there you do not find words of knowledge. Proverbs __14__ : __7__

5. My child, do not forget my teaching, but let your heart keep my commandments. Proverbs __3__ : __1__

6. My child, keep my words and store up my commandments with you. Proverbs __7__ : __1__

7. No one finds security by wickedness, but the root of the righteous will never be moved. Proverbs __12__ : __3__

8. Lay aside immaturity, and live, and walk in the way of insight. Proverbs __9__ : __6__

9. The fear of the LORD is the beginning of knowledge; fools despise wisdom and instruction. Proverbs __1__ : __7__

 Summer Sunday School Puzzles, © 2008 Abingdon Press

Puzzle 83

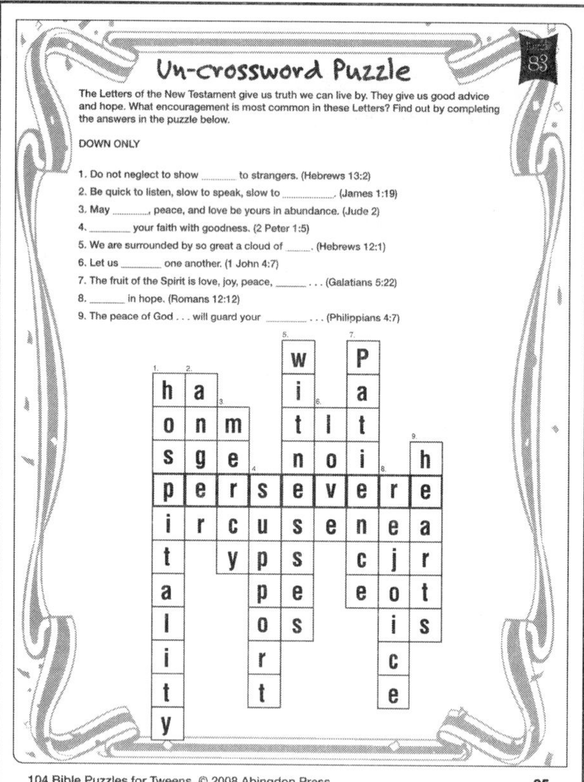

104 Bible Puzzles for Tweens, © 2008 Abingdon Press   95

Puzzle 85

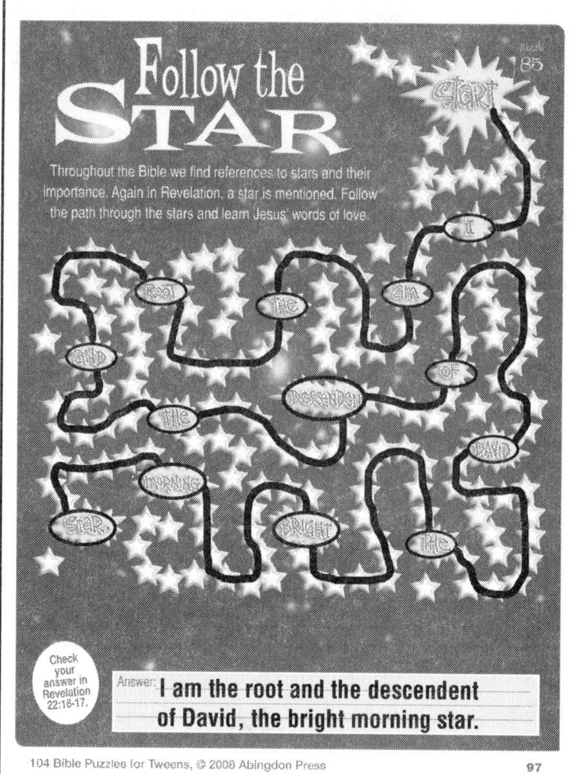

104 Bible Puzzles for Tweens, © 2008 Abingdon Press   97

Puzzle 84

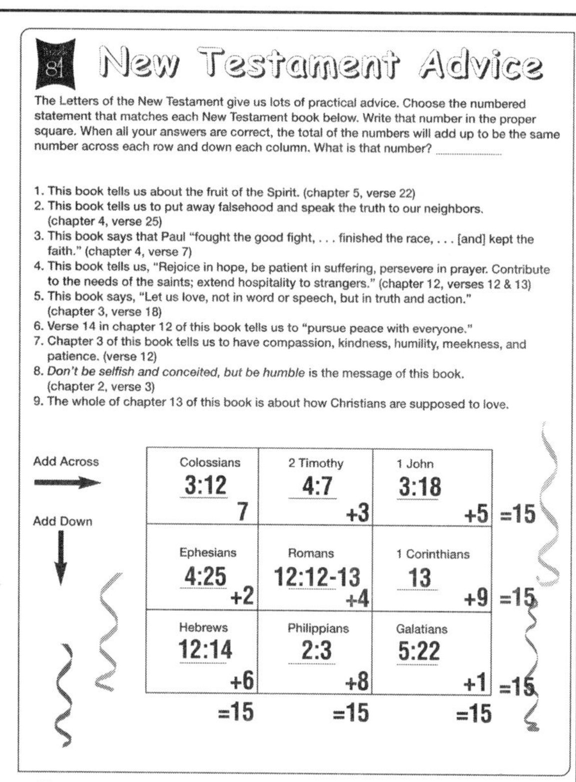

	Colossians 3:12	2 Timothy 4:7	1 John 3:18	
	7	+3	+5	=15
	Ephesians 4:25	Romans 12:12-13	1 Corinthians 13	
	+2	+4	+9	=15
	Hebrews 12:14	Philippians 2:3	Galatians 5:22	
	+6	+8	+1	=15
	=15	=15	=15	

96   Summer Sunday School Puzzles, © 2008 Abingdon Press

Puzzle 86

I AM THE
ALPHA
AND THE
OMEGA
SAYS THE
LORD GOD

Puzzle 87

Puzzle 89

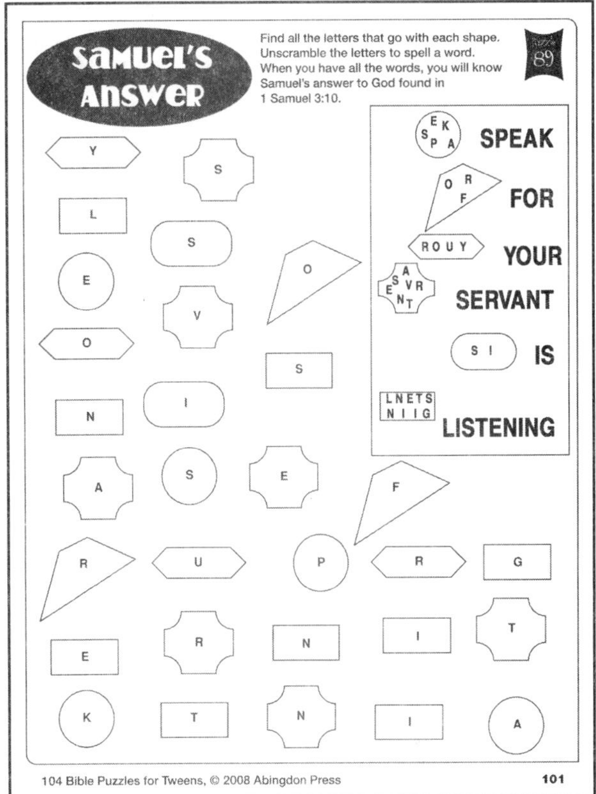

Puzzle 88

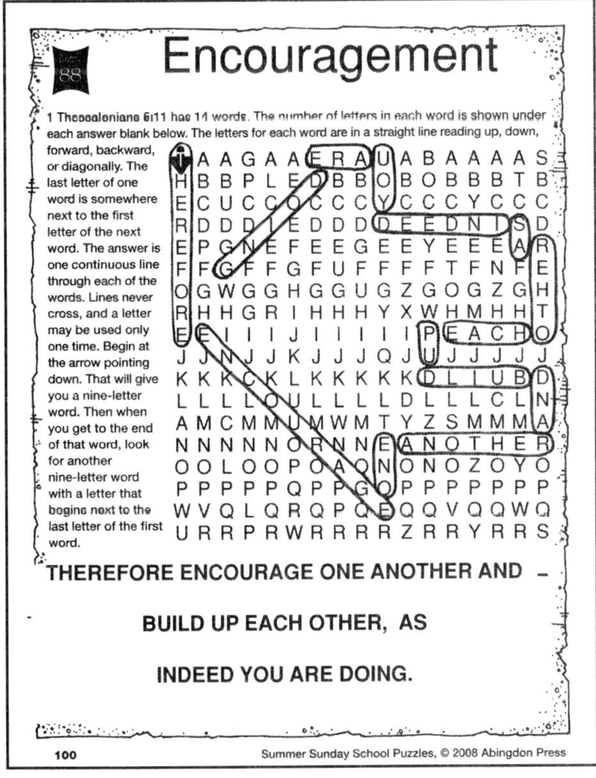

Puzzle 90

1. OT	6. NT
2. NT	7. NT
3. OT	8. OT
4. OT	9. OT
5. OT	10. NT

Puzzle 91

When he saw their faith he said friend your sins are forgiven you Luke 5:20

Puzzle 92

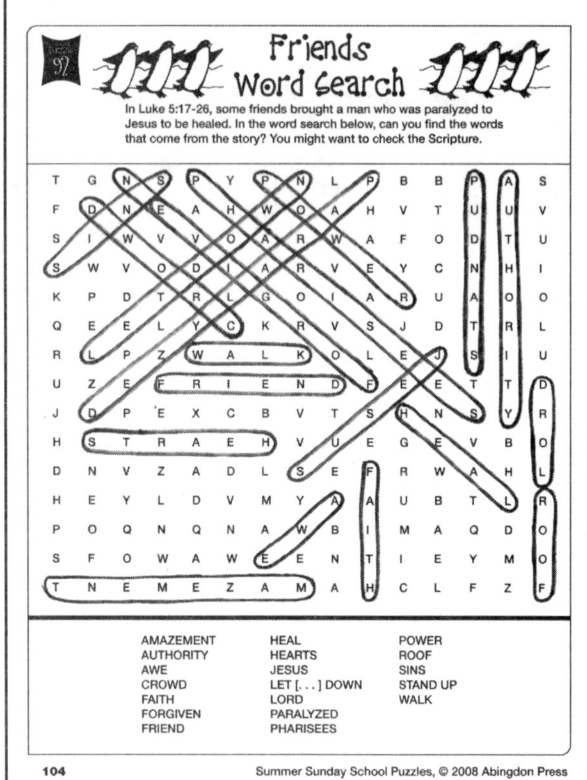

104   Summer Sunday School Puzzles, © 2008 Abingdon Press

Puzzle 95

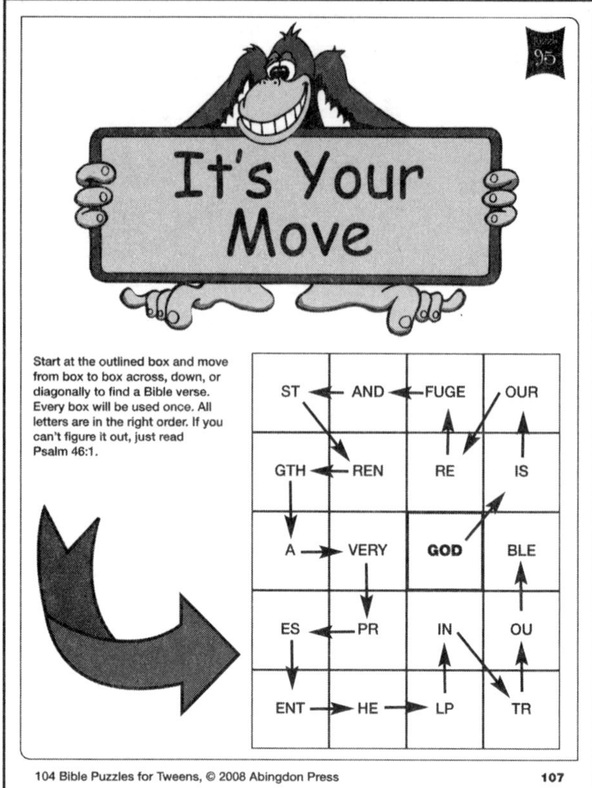

104 Bible Puzzles for Tweens, © 2008 Abingdon Press   107

Puzzle 96

T H E L O R D I N D E E D I S G O D

Puzzle 93

1. Abel	7. Absalom
2. Isaac	8. Jesus
3. Laban	9. John the Baptist
4. Judah	10. Lazarus
5. Aaron	11. Eunice
6. Boaz	

Puzzle 94

I AM REMINDED OF YOUR SINCERE FAITH, A FAITH THAT LIVED FIRST IN YOUR GRANDMOTHER LOIS AND YOUR MOTHER EUNICE AND NOW, I AM SURE, LIVES IN YOU. 2 TIMOTHY 1:5

Puzzle 97

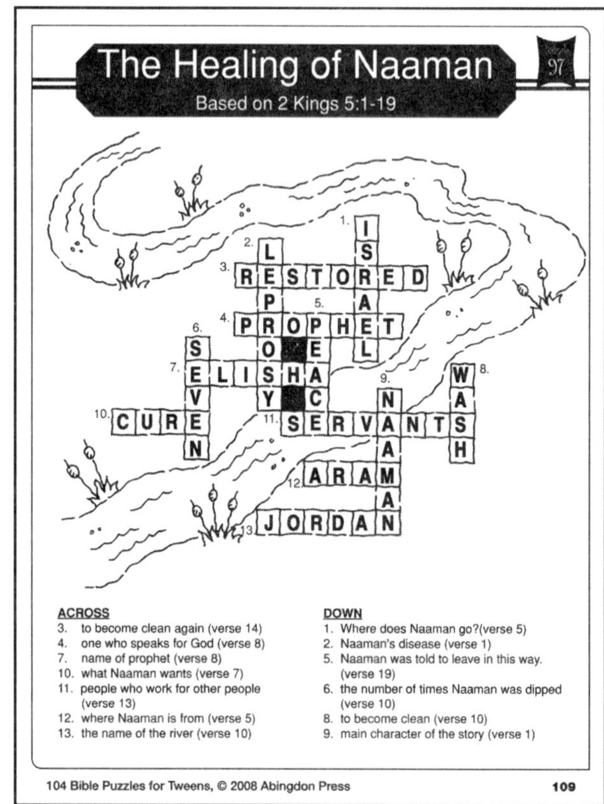

ACROSS
3. to become clean again (verse 14)
4. one who speaks for God (verse 8)
7. name of prophet (verse 8)
10. what Naaman wants (verse 7)
11. people who work for other people (verse 13)
12. where Naaman is from (verse 5)
13. the name of the river (verse 10)

DOWN
1. Where does Naaman go? (verse 5)
2. Naaman's disease (verse 1)
5. Naaman was told to leave in this way. (verse 19)
6. the number of times Naaman was dipped (verse 10)
8. to become clean (verse 10)
9. main character of the story (verse 1)

104 Bible Puzzles for Tweens, © 2008 Abingdon Press   109

Puzzle 98

Why couldn't Naaman pay Elisha
for the miracle of healing?

Miracles are received by grace.

Puzzle 101

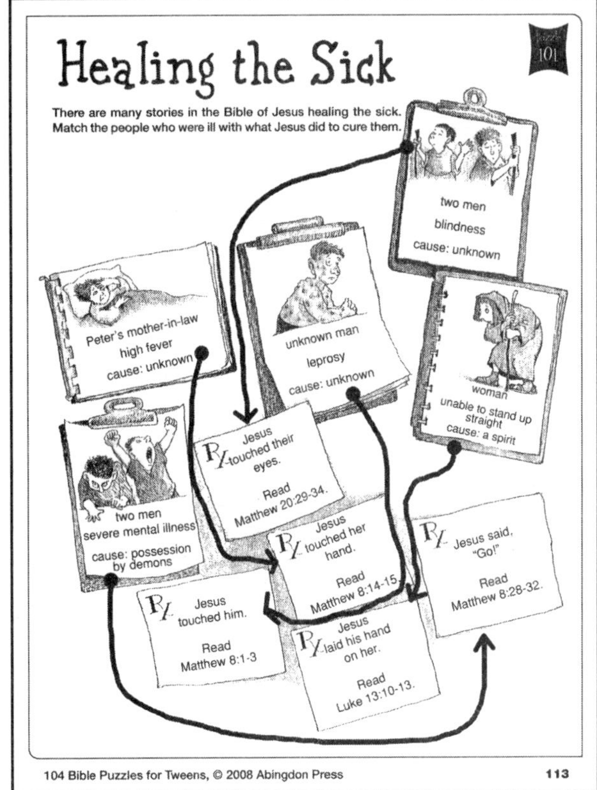

Puzzle 99

DAVID
DORCAS
STEPHEN
NOAH
HEROD
DANIEL
LUKE
EVE
ELIZABETH
HOSEA
ADAM
MARTHA
ABRAHAM
MOSES
SOLOMON

Puzzle 100:

DO NOT LET YOUR HEARTS
BE TROUBLED.
BELIEVE IN GOD,
BELIEVE ALSO IN ME.

Puzzle 102

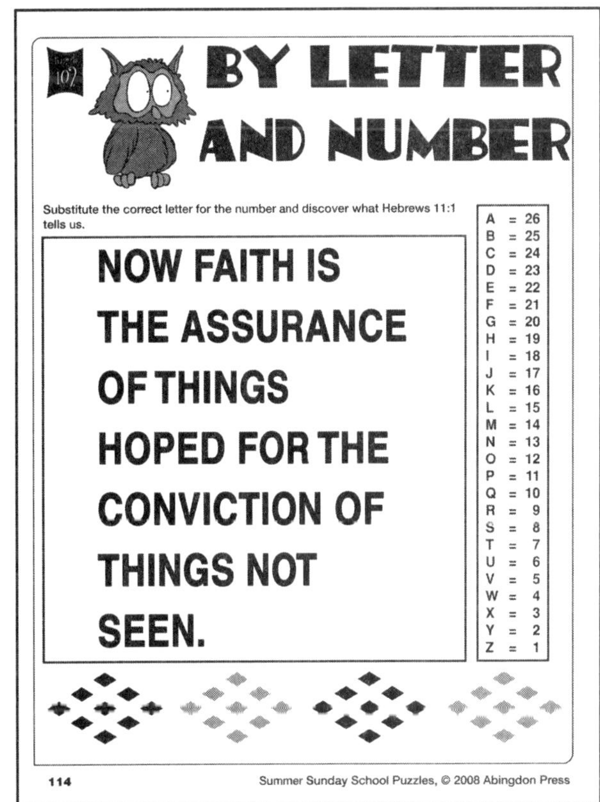

Puzzle 103

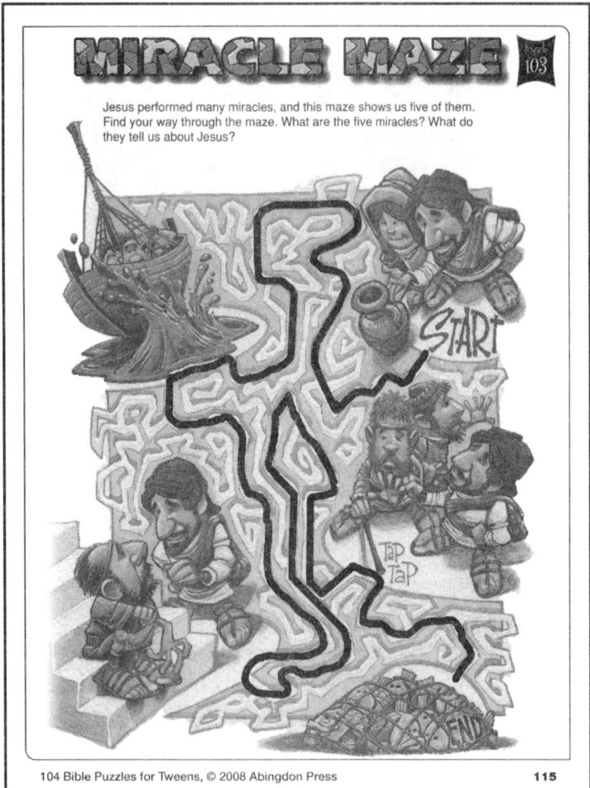

What are the five miracles?
1) Jesus turns water into wine. 2) Jesus calms the storm. 3) Jesus heals a withered hand on the Sabbath. 4) Jesus heals two blind men. 5) The disciples' net is filled.

What do they tell us about Jesus?
This question is for discussion.

Puzzle 104

Simon Peter + Thomas + Nathanael,
+ the 2 sons of Zebedee, + 2 other disciples = **7**.

25 x 2 + 60 - 10 = **100** yards off shore.

277 - 155 + 35 - 4 = **153** fish.

33 divided by 3 - 8 = **3**. It was the **third** time that Jesus appeared to the disciples after he was raised from the dead.

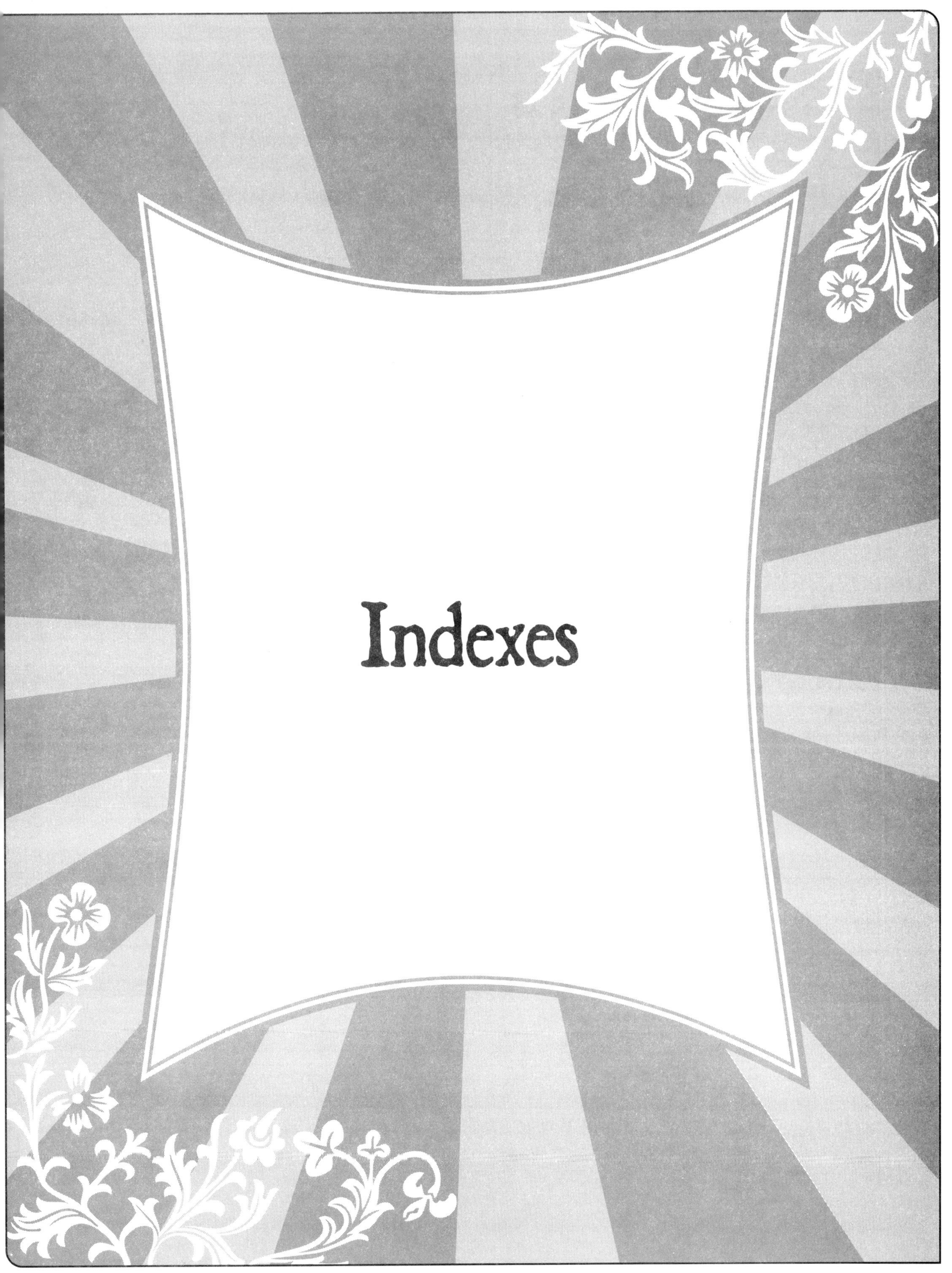

Indexes

Topical Index

Scripture Index

Old Testament

Mixed Old Testament Scripture References

Mixed Old and New Testament References

Note: The following puzzles are not related to any specific Scriptures:

**Additional Puzzles for Summer Sessions

Credits

p. 16: *Exploring Faith: Preteen Student Magazine,*
Fall 2001, © 2001 Cokesbury.
p. 18, 19: *The Promised Land: An Old Testament Activity
Book,* © 1999 Abingdon Press.
p. 20: *Exploring Faith: Bible Brain Pak,* Fall 2006,
© 2006 Cokesbury.
p. 35: *Bible Zone Live: Older Elementary, Teacher's Guide,*
© 2003 Abingdon Press.
p. 37: *Exploring Faith: Bible Brain Pak,* Winter 2006-07,
© 2006 Cokesbury.
p. 39, 40: *Exploring Faith: Bible Brain Pak,* Winter
2005-06, © 2005 Cokesbury.
p. 47: *Exploring Faith: Older Elementary, Student,* Summer
2001, Leaflet 5, © 2001 Cokesbury.
p. 50: *Exploring Faith: Bible Brain Pak,* Summer 2006,
© 2006 Cokesbury.
p. 65: *Symbols of Faith: Teaching Images of the Christian
Faith,* © Abingdon Press.
p. 67, 79, 81: *Exploring Faith: Bible Brain Pak,*
Spring 2005, © 2004 Cokesbury.
p. 70: *Exploring Faith: Preteen Class Pak,* Spring 2003,
© 2002 Cokesbury.
p. 75, 87: *Exploring Faith: Bible Brain Pak,* Spring 2006,
© 2005 Cokesbury.
p. 77, 82: *One Room Sunday School: Reproducible
Activities,* Spring 1998, © 1997 Abingdon Press.
p. 91: *One Room Sunday School: Reproducible Activities,*
Summer 2006, © 2003, 2006 Abingdon Press.
p. 92: *One Room Sunday School: Reproducible Activities,*
Summer 2005, © 2005 Abingdon Press.
p. 95: *Exploring Faith: FaithZine, Summer 2005,*
© 2005 Cokesbury.
p. 97: *Exploring Faith: Bible Brain Pak, Summer 2004,*
© 2004 Cokesbury.
p. 99: James H. Ritchie, Jr., Ed.D. *Live B.I.G., 11-13
Leader's Guide,* Winter 2006-07, © 2006 Abingdon Press.
p. 109: *One Room Sunday School: Reproducible Activities,*
Fall 2004, © 2004 Abingdon Press.
p. 110: *Exploring Faith: Tweens in Transition, Teacher,*
Summer 2007, © 2007 Cokesbury.
p. 113: *One Room Sunday School: Reproducible Activities,*
Winter 2004-05, © 2004 Abingdon Press.
p. 115: *Exploring Faith: Preteen, Student Magazine,*
Summer 2001, © 2001 Cokesbury.

Art Credits

p. 8, 43, 86: Randy Wollenmann
pp. 9, 14, 45, 61: Dennis Jones
p. 15, 55: Bob Jones
p. 16, 115: Dennis Jones, © 2001 Cokesbury
p. 17, 51: Liquid Library
p. 18: Robert S. Jones, © 1999 Abingdon Press
p. 19: Paige Easter
p. 20: Bob Jones, © 2006 Cokesbury
p. 28 (Deborah): Francis Phillipps / Linden Artists,
© 2001 Cokesbury
p. 28 (David): Francis Phillipps / Linden Artists,
© 2003 Cokesbury
p. 28 (Abigail, Bathsheba, Nathan): Francis Phillipps /
Linden Artists, © 2004 Cokesbury
p. 28 (Saul): Francis Phillipps / Linden Artists,
© 2005 Cokesbury
p. 28 (Jonathan, Samuel, Solomon): Francis Phillipps /
Linden Artists, © 2006 Cokesbury
p. 28 (Moses): Marcy Ramsey / Portfolio Solutions,
© 2007 Cokesbury
p. 35: Jim Padgett, © 2003 Abingdon Press
p. 38: Randy Wollenmann, © 2008 Cokesbury
p. 39, 40, 75: Paige Easter, © 2005 Cokesbury
p. 47: Peter Stevenson / Linden Artists, © 2001 Cokesbury
p. 50: Dennis Jones, © 2006 Cokesbury
p. 58: Megan Jeffrey, © 2006
p. 67: Randy Wollenmann, © 2004 Cokesbury
p. 70: Randy Wollenmann, © 2002 Cokesbury
p. 77: Randy Wollenmann, ©1997 Abingdon Press
p. 79: Paige Easter, © 2004 Cokesbury
p. 81: Kathie Kelleher / Portfolio Solutions,
© 2000 Cokesbury
p. 82: Doug Jones, © 1997 Abingdon Press
p. 87: Randy Wollenmann, © 2005 Cokesbury
p. 91: Susan Harrison, © 2003, 2006 Abingdon Press
p. 92: Dennis Jones, © 2005 Abingdon Press
p. 94: © 2007 ColoringPlanet.com
p. 97: Dennis Jones, © 2004 Cokesbury
p. 99: Amy Reid, © 2006 Abingdon Press
p. 109: Terry Sirrell, © 2004 Abingdon Press
p. 113: Robert W. Alley / Publishers' Graphics,
© 2004 Abingdon Press